Responding to New Realities in Funding

Larry L. Leslie, *Editor*

NEW DIRECTIONS FOR INSTITUTIONAL RESEARCH
Sponsored by the Association for Institutional Research
MARVIN W. PETERSON, PATRICK T. TERENZINI
Editors-in-Chief

Number 43, September 1984

Paperback sourcebooks in
The Jossey-Bass Higher Education Series

Jossey-Bass Inc., Publishers
San Francisco • Washington • London

Larry L. Leslie (Ed.).
Responding to New Realities in Funding.
New Directions for Institutional Research, no. 43.
Volume XI, number 3.
San Francisco: Jossey-Bass, 1984

New Directions for Institutional Research Series
Marvin W. Peterson, Patrick T. Terenzini, *Editors-in-Chief*

Copyright © 1984 by Jossey-Bass Inc., Publishers
          and
          Jossey-Bass Limited

Copyright under International, Pan American, and Universal
Copyright Conventions. All rights reserved. No part of
this issue may be reproduced in any form — except for brief
quotation (not to exceed 500 words) in a review or professional
work — without permission in writing from the publishers.

New Directions for Institutional Research (publication number
USPS 098-830) is published quarterly by Jossey-Bass Inc.,
Publishers, and is sponsored by the Association for Institutional
Research. The volume and issue numbers above are included for
the convenience of libraries. Second-class postage rates paid at
San Francisco, California, and at additional mailing offices.

Correspondence:
Subscriptions, single-issue orders, change of address notices, undelivered
copies, and other correspondence should be sent to Subscriptions,
Jossey-Bass Inc., Publishers, 433 California Street, San Francisco
California 94104.

Editorial correspondence should be sent to the Editor-in-Chief,
Marvin W. Peterson, Center for the Study of Higher Education,
University of Michigan, Ann Arbor, Michigan 48109, or
Patrick T. Terenzini, Office of Institutional Research, SUNY,
Albany, New York 12222.

Library of Congress Catalogue Card Number LC 83-82729
International Standard Serial Number ISSN 0271-0579
International Standard Book Number ISBN 87589-776-2

Cover art by Willi Baum
Manufactured in the United States of America

Ordering Information

The paperback sourcebooks listed below are published quarterly and can be ordered either by subscription or single-copy.

Subscriptions cost $35.00 per year for institutions, agencies, and libraries. Individuals can subscribe at the special rate of $25.00 per year *if payment is by personal check*. (Note that the full rate of $35.00 applies if payment is by institutional check, even if the subscription is designated for an individual.) Standing orders are accepted. Subscriptions normally begin with the first of the four sourcebooks in the current publication year of the series. When ordering, please indicate if you prefer your subscription to begin with the first issue of the *coming* year.

Single copies are available at $8.95 when payment accompanies order, and *all single-copy orders under $25.00 must include payment*. (California, New Jersey, New York, and Washington, D.C., residents please include appropriate sales tax.) For billed orders, cost per copy is $8.95 plus postage and handling. (Prices subject to change without notice.)

Bulk orders (ten or more copies) of any individual sourcebook are available at the following discounted prices: 10–49 copies, $8.05 each; 50–100 copies, $7.15 each; over 100 copies, *inquire*. Sales tax and postage and handling charges apply as for single copy orders.

To ensure correct and prompt delivery, all orders must give either the *name of an individual* or an *official purchase order number*. Please submit your order as follows:

Subscriptions: specify series and year subscription is to begin.
Single Copies: specify sourcebook code (such as, IR8) and first two words of title.

Mail orders for United States and Possessions, Latin America, Canada, Japan, Australia, and New Zealand to:
    Jossey-Bass Inc., Publishers
    433 California Street
    San Francisco, California 94104

Mail orders for all other parts of the world to:
    Jossey-Bass Limited
    28 Banner Street
    London EC1Y 8QE

New Directions for Institutional Research Series
Marvin W. Peterson, Patrick T. Terenzini
Editors-in-Chief

IR1 *Evaluating Institutions for Accountability,* Howard R. Bowen
IR2 *Assessing Faculty Effort,* James I. Doi
IR3 *Toward Affirmative Action,* Lucy W. Sells
IR4 *Organizing Nontraditional Study,* Samuel Baskin

IR5   *Evaluating Statewide Boards,* Robert O. Berdahl
IR6   *Assuring Academic Progress Without Growth,* Allan M. Cartter
IR7   *Responding to Changing Human Resource Needs,* Paul Heist, Jonathan R. Warren
IR8   *Measuring and Increasing Academic Productivity,* Robert A. Wallhaus
IR9   *Assessing Computer-Based System Models,* Thomas R. Mason
IR10 *Examining Departmental Management,* James Smart, James Montgomery
IR11 *Allocating Resources Among Departments,* Paul L. Dressel, Lou Anna Kimsey Simon
IR12 *Benefiting from Interinstitutional Research,* Marvin W. Peterson
IR13 *Applying Analytic Methods to Planning and Management,* David S. P. Hopkins, Roger G. Schroeder
IR14 *Protecting Individual Rights to Privacy in Higher Education,* Alton L. Taylor
IR15 *Appraising Information Needs of Decision Makers,* Carl R. Adams
IR16 *Increasing the Public Accountability of Higher Education,* John K. Folger
IR17 *Analyzing and Constructing Cost,* Meredith A. Gonyea
IR18 *Employing Part-Time Faculty,* David W. Leslie
IR19 *Using Goals in Research and Planning,* Robert Fenske
IR20 *Evaluating Faculty Performance and Vitality,* Wayne C. Kirschling
IR21 *Developing a Total Marketing Plan,* John A. Lucas
IR22 *Examining New Trends in Administrative Computing,* E. Michael Staman
IR23 *Professional Development for Institutional Research,* Robert G. Cope
IR24 *Planning Rational Retrenchment,* Alfred L. Cooke
IR25 *The Impact of Student Financial Aid on Institutions,* Joe B. Henry
IR26 *The Autonomy of Public Colleges,* Paul L. Dressel
IR27 *Academic Program Evaluation,* Eugene C. Craven
IR28 *Academic Planning for the 1980s,* Richard B. Heydinger
IR29 *Institutional Assessment for Self-Improvement,* Richard I. Miller
IR30 *Coping with Faculty Reduction,* Stephen R. Hample
IR31 *Evaluation of Management and Planning Systems,* Nick L. Poulton
IR32 *Increasing the Use of Program Evaluation,* Jack Lindquist
IR33 *Effective Planned Change Strategies,* G. Melvin Hipps
IR34 *Qualitative Methods for Institutional Research,* Eileen Kuhns, S. V. Martorana
IR35 *Information Technology: Advances and Applications,* Bernard Sheehan
IR36 *Studying Student Attrition,* Ernest T. Pascarella
IR37 *Using Research for Strategic Planning,* Norman P. Uhl
IR38 *The Politics and Pragmatics of Institutional Research,* James W. Firnberg, William F. Lasher
IR39 *Applying Methods and Techniques of Futures Research,* James L. Morrison, William L. Renfro, Wayne I. Boucher
IR40 *College Faculty: Versatile Human Resources in a Period of Constraint,* Roger G. Baldwin, Robert T. Blackburn
IR41 *Determining the Effectiveness of Campus Services,* Robert A. Scott
IR42 *Issues in Pricing Undergraduate Education,* Larry H. Litten

Contents

Editor's Notes 1
Larry L. Leslie

Chapter 1. The New Strategies: Roots, Context, and Overview 5
Anthony W. Morgan
The new financing strategies may be conceptualized in two fundamental ways: rational calculation approaches and market interaction approaches.

Chapter 2. Formula Budgeting: The Fourth Decade 21
Paul T. Brinkman
Roughly twenty-six states allocate resources to higher education primarily on a formula basis. Many changes in formulas are being witnessed.

Chapter 3. New Approaches to Incentive Financing 45
Richard H. Allen
Within many states and institutions, efforts are being expanded to provide incentives for better financial management.

Chapter 4. Budgeting Strategies Under Conditions of Decline 67
Kenneth P. Mortimer, Barbara E. Taylor
On college campuses, the forms of response to budgeting shortfalls are numerous and ubiquitous.

Chapter 5. Bringing the Issues Together 87
Larry L. Leslie
A synthesis of Chapters One through Four covers the full range of recent financing changes. The strategies fit together as envisaged by Morgan.

Index 101

The Association for Institutional Research was created in 1966 to benefit, assist, and advance research leading to improved understanding, planning, and operation of institutions of higher education. Publication policy is set by its Publications Board.

PUBLICATIONS BOARD
Stephen R. Hample (Chairperson), Montana State University
Ellen E. Chaffee, National Center for Higher Education Management Systems
Jean J. Endo, University of Colorado at Boulder
Cameron L. Fincher, University of Georgia
Richard B. Heydinger, University of Minnesota
Penny A. Wallhaus, Illinois Community College Board

EX-OFFICIO MEMBERS OF THE PUBLICATIONS BOARD
Charles F. Elton, University of Kentucky
Elizabeth F. Fox, University of Alabama in Birmingham
Gerald W. McLaughlin, Virginia Polytechnic Institute & State University
Marvin W. Peterson, University of Michigan
Patrick T. Terenzini, State University of New York at Albany

EDITORIAL ADVISORY BOARD
All members of the Publications Board and:
Frederick E. Balderston, University of California, Berkeley
Howard R. Bowen, Claremont Graduate School
Roberta D. Brown, Arkansas College
Lyman A. Glenny, University of California, Berkeley (retired)
David S. P. Hopkins, Stanford University
Roger G. Schroeder, University of Minnesota
Robert J. Silverman, Ohio State University
Martin A. Trow, University of California, Berkeley

For information about the Association for Institutional Research, write:

>AIR Executive Office
>314 Stone Building
>Florida State University
>Tallahassee, FL 32306
>(904) 644-4470

Editor's Notes

In a more quiet time on our college campuses, the feeling of well-being that hung lightly on the classroom air pervaded also the faculty office, the union lounge, the corridors of Old Main, and even the campus budget office, by whatever name it was called. Our institutions were at an interlude: We had met the challenge of growth of the Golden Decade; our buildings were built, the faculty were hired, and it was time to pause, reflect, and consolidate our gains.

It was not the time for something new. Our energies were spent and the need was to bask a little in the sunlight we had helped to create. Called for was a nurturing of the status quo: to conduct our business as usual, to develop our routines, and to institutionalize our procedures.

We knew that the calm would be brief; as with all such lulls, a new crisis would soon be upon us. And it was.

We had ample warning that it was coming. For almost a decade we had known that it was enrollment decline, not prosperity, that was "just around the corner." What we had not foreseen was that the new enrollment era would be accompanied by the worst recession in forty years. Even if we had anticipated the recession, it is doubtful that we would have assessed accurately the full effects of the interaction of enrollment and state revenue decline. Now it is not so quiet in our campus budget office.

But times of challenge are also times of opportunity. One does not tamper with smoothly running machinery—or organizations: If it is not broken, do not fix it. Mandates for change occur only when all is not well, and the opportunity provided by such stress is almost as great on the way down as it was on the way up.

The prospect of enrollment decline for most institutions and the reality of it for some, interacting with the effects of the recent recession upon these institutions' revenues, have created fertile ground for innovations in financing. Governors, state legislatures, and state boards have pressed institutions to find new ways of stretching dollars farther. Institutions sometimes have petitioned state agents for increased autonomy and flexibility in raising and spending revenues; often, institutional leaders have persuaded, ordered, or cajoled their financial staff to alter traditional resource allocation modes.

This volume looks at the higher education resource allocation process; it examines new allocation strategies, reflects on their successes and failures, and comments upon their implications for the long term. In each chapter, the implications for institutional research are at the forefront.

First, Anthony W. Morgan provides a broad perspective for viewing the resource allocation process. As executive assistant to the president at the University of Utah, Morgan has been involved both in negotiating for funds (in a state where revenues have been sharply curtailed while enrollment pressures have continued to increase) and in finding new ways to allocate funds within the university. His earlier efforts to conceptualize budgeting strategies (Morgan, 1977-1978) and to contrast costs in higher education and the health care industry (Morgan, 1983) are considered seminal works. His chapter describes the context of the current flurry of activity and affords the reader a means of interpreting and assessing resource allocation strategies.

In the second chapter, Paul T. Brinkman examines new developments in the major vehicle for state allocations to institutions. At last count, formula budgets were the primary allocation tool in twenty-six states, and Brinkman, senior associate at the National Center for Higher Education Management Systems (NCHEMS), has been leading a national costing effort funded by the National Institute of Education (NIE). He has also emerged nationally as a prolific writer and expert analyst of costing in higher education. For example, his monograph on marginal costing (Allen and Brinkman, 1983) has been widely recognized as the standard work on this subject. Costing, of course, is the process that underlies funding formulas and the changes made in them.

Richard H. Allen, in Chapter Three, writes on the use of incentives in higher education financing. Allen's professional experience has placed him at the center of national financing developments. He has served as an executive budget analyst for higher education in Michigan and as a representative of NCHEMS, and he is now the state higher education finance officer in Colorado, currently the national "hot spot" in incentive financing.

In Chapter Four, Kenneth P. Mortimer and Barbara E. Taylor utilize a just-completed study for the Lilly Endowment to discuss the various ways by which institutions have responded to revenue shortfalls. Mortimer's ERIC-AAHE monograph (Mortimer and Tierney, 1979), *The Three R's of the Eighties: Reduction, Reallocation, and Retrenchment*, established him as one of the most insightful observers and commentators on the topic of reactions to fiscal stress. Mortimer, professor and senior scientist at Pennsylvania State University's Center for the Study of Higher Education, chairs the National Institute of Education's recently appointed panel on "The Condition of Excellence in American Higher Education." Taylor is assistant to the vice-chancellor for academic programs, policy, and planning, State University of New York. She served as a research associate on the project on the role of trustees in academic program and personnel development funded by Ford and Exxon.

In the fifth and last chapter, the editor synthesizes the previous chapters, adds his own commentary to the topics addressed, fills in some important gaps on the general topic, considers the successes and failures of the new strategies, and makes suggestions as to additional references. The editor teaches higher education finance, conducts the annual national finance conference, and is author of approximately seventy papers and monographs on financing topics.

Larry L. Leslie
Editor

References

Allen, R., and Brinkman, P. *Marginal Costing Techniques for Higher Education.* Boulder, Colo.: National Center for Higher Education Management Systems, 1983.

Morgan, A. W. "Resource Allocation Reforms: Marginal Utility Analysis and Zero-Based Budgeting in Higher Education." *Higher Education Review,* 1977–1978, *1*, 1–17.

Morgan, A. W. "Cost as a Policy Issue: Lessons from the Health Care Sector." *Journal of Higher Education,* 1983, *54*, 279–293.

Mortimer, K. P., and Tierney, M. *The Three R's of the Eighties: Reduction, Reallocation, and Retrenchment.* AAHE-ERIC/Higher Education Report No. 4. Washington, D.C.: American Association for Higher Education, 1979.

Larry L. Leslie is professor of higher education and director of the Center for the Study of Higher Education at the University of Arizona.

"New" strategies for resource allocation are, like their predecessors, based on certain root assumptions about decision making and on allocation models that flow from these assumptions.

The New Strategies: Roots, Context, and Overview

Anthony W. Morgan

How to distribute funds among competing claims is one of life's enduring questions. Vern Lewis (1952), one of the early proponents of bringing increased rationality to resource allocation in the public sector, repeated the basic distribution question posed by political scientist V. O. Key (1940) a decade earlier: "On what basis shall it be decided to allocate x dollars to Activity A instead of allocating them to Activity B?" (Lewis, 1952, p. 42). Lewis's question is as vital an issue in public policy discussions today as it was then, despite the fact that theoreticians and practitioners alike have developed many theories and strategies to cope with this vexing issue.

    This chapter examines, in a succinct and simplified form, the steady stream of theories and practices that have been developed over the past two or three decades in response to the issue posed by Lewis and others. Most of the strategies for resource allocation, be they old or new, are rooted in a limited number of key assumptions about how such decisions should be made. These root assumptions, and the various resource allocation models that flow from them, carry associated strengths and limitations. Any particular strategy, based upon the models, then, carries with it some measure of these systemic limitations.

Thus, if we understand better the basic theoretical building blocks of resource allocation strategies, we will be in a better position to evaluate new strategies as they are proposed and debated. For example, if other strategies using similar theoretical building blocks were tried in the past, we can ask if the current strategies or conditions differ sufficiently to warrant some measure of optimism as to their success and some reason for investing in them.

Resource Allocation Decisions: Root Assumptions

For the purposes of this chapter, two basic sets of root assumptions, or paradigms, are identified as a basis for discussing selected decision models of resource allocation. This essentially dichotomous view of decision theory is taken largely from the works of economist Charles Lindblom (1977) and political scientist Aaron Wildavsky (1979), although it is a view shared by many authors.

The first set of root assumptions is called the *rational calculation* view; it encompasses the notion that resource allocation decisions can be made best by relatively few individuals using an intellectual calculus for collecting and analyzing relatively objective information. Allocation models flowing from rational calculation assumptions include, but are not limited to, various goal models, investment or marginal utility analysis, and cost reimbursement strategies.

The second set of root assumptions, *market interaction*, is evident in both economic and political theory. Its premise is basically that widely dispersed decisions arrived at through market or political interaction produce results that satisfy the most people. Interest-group bargaining and various competitive market strategies involving the restructuring of incentives flow from these premises.

Figure 1 summarizes these root assumptions and allocation models as well as particular strategies that have evolved from the models. Some of the particular strategies listed incorporate components of more than one model and must be assessed on that basis. The purpose of this figure is illustrative rather than strictly taxonomical. The discussion that follows amplifies these root assumptions, their allocation models, and some of the past and present resource allocation strategies that flow from them.

Rational Calculation. The attraction of developing and applying rational calculation to the problem of allocating funds in higher education is rooted, as James March has noted, in what we believe to be intelligent choice. That is, we in contemporary occidental cultures assume that human choice does in fact significantly influence outcomes of behavior and, furthermore, we assume that, in making choices, we can and should

Figure 1. Resource Allocation Strategies

Root Assumptions	Allocation Model	"Old" Strategies	"New" Strategies	Strengths	Weaknesses
Rational Calculation	Goals (Rational-deductive)	Planning-Programming-Budgeting System (PPBS) Management by objectives (MBO)	Strategic planning	• Focus on ends • Relating means to ends • Sense of direction	• Assumption of knowledge • Consensus • Flexibility/opportunism
	Investment (Marginal utility)	Benefit-cost analysis Zero-based budgeting (ZBB)	Performance budgeting	• Focus on results • Objectivity • Manageable scope	• Valid criteria • Reliable measures • Ad hoc nature
	Cost reimbursement	Performance budgeting (1940s, 1950s) Formula budgeting	Marginal-cost formulas	• Simplicity • Routinization • Equity	• Status quo • Lack of planning
Market Interaction	Interest-group bargaining	Logrolling	Domain defense	• Political rationality • Feasibility	• Nondirectional • Status quo • Tyranny of majority
	Structuring incentives	Vouchers Health maintenance organizations (HMOs) "Every tub"	Responsibility-center budgeting Incentive planning	• Responsiveness • Competition • Decisions close to action	• Absence of market conditions • Nondirectional • Lack of central controls

define our "objectives," "preferences," "values," or other similar labels for what March calls the "pre-existence of purpose." Purpose, then, serves as *the* guiding criterion of choice, and, once settled upon, it is subject to the technology of choice—namely, the search for alternatives, the assembly and analysis of information regarding those alternatives, and the selection of the "best" alternatives based on systematically relating the consequence of proposed allocations to established objectives (Cohen and March, 1974; March and Olsen, 1976).

This view of choice, permeated as it is by the canons of rationality, undergirds most of the rational calculation models of resource allocation. It strikes a responsive chord at both individual and organizational levels and serves for many people as a model or norm against which "good" decision making is measured.

While many rational calculation models could be cited as illustrative of this general approach to resource allocation, the three treated here have sparked several of the planning and budgeting strategies most commonly used or proposed in the past.

Goals. This first strategy, derived from what Braybrooke and Lindblom (1963) call the "rational-deductive" ideal, is to develop goals or general principles from which specific planning and budgeting decisions can be made. Some economists have attempted to refine this strategy by constructing a welfare function or a scale of quantitative values against which alternative uses of resources can be evaluated.

Since it is difficult to derive specific policies from very broad, general principles or goals, many goal strategies focus on developing intermediate working principles in order to move towards greater specificity. The Planning-Programming-Budgeting System (PPBS), introduced in the federal government in the 1960s, adopted this approach by structuring a system that included general, long-term goals and more immediate objectives tied to those goals. Management by objectives (MBO) strategies have also attempted to merge overall organizational goals with operating-level goals or objectives.

Most recently, strategic planning has emerged as the "new" strategy for resource allocation in the 1980s. While there are many varieties of strategic planning, which incorporate elements of other models besides the goal model, two examples are cited here. The first illustration comes from Kotler and Murphy's (1981) classic marketing approach. This strategy emphasizes goal formulation and uses environmental and resource analysis as a planning and control mechanism: "The purpose of developing a clear set of institutional goals is precisely to keep the organization from drifting into an uncertain future. . . . Without goals, whatever the organization does or achieves can be considered acceptable; there is no standard for planning or control" (pp. 477-478).

Goals can be developed "top down" or "bottom up" or in various combinations. Kotler and Murphy opt for a fairly strong top-down mode consistent with the classical goal model.

A second example is George Keller's (1983) recent work, which incorporates a much wider range of strategies including elements of market interaction models (both political and economic). While both examples of strategic planning incorporate "feedback" loops that allow for modification of goals based on changes in environmental conditions, the approaches are predominately goal-based and rooted in rational calculation.

Goal-based strategies are essentially deductive logic approaches to resource allocation. The goals may be formulated by a few individuals or a few groups (top down) or by many (bottom up), but, once formed, the goals provide the basis of planning and control. Bottom-up goal formulation strategies, such as the Michigan State University case (Freeman and Simpson, 1980), pose a special problem of aggregating and integrating individual preferences (Hoenack and Berg, 1980).

One of the central weaknesses of goal strategies is that you may be wrong. The model requires some smart folks (assumption of knowledge) and a relatively predictable environment. Market economies are littered with the corpses of companies that were wrong or that were inflexibly wedded to goals and targets tied to yesterday's opportunities. Goal strategies also require consensus within an organization, at least at top echelons. Consensus is easy at high levels of generality (such as in quality teaching) and under conditions of growth where there are often some rewards for everyone. Consensus is more difficult when specificity of goals is required or when resources are constrained to the point where the psychology of the "territorial imperative" predominates (Morgan, 1982).

If the strategic planners and leaders are correct in their assessment of opportunities in the environment, however, great shall be their reward. Thus, many institutional leaders play a fairly conservative strategic game, opting in many cases for retention of a comprehensive array of programs and for conservative management strategies (Cameron, 1983).

Resource Allocation as Investment Decisions. A second model flowing from rational calculation assumptions comes from the field of microeconomics and from budgeting in the private sector. Here the model is an investment decision where such economic terms as "marginal utility analysis" and "benefit-cost ratio" become the tools and nomenclature of the trade. Basically, the investment (or "marginal utility") model has three components: (1) dividing available resources into increments so that assessments and comparisons can be made about specific increments (or decrements) rather than about general totals; (2) assessing the returns or benefits associated with each increment; and (3) comparing the relative benefits within and across categories of expenditures (Morgan, 1977-1978).

Dividing resources into increments is not just a matter of manageability. From a theoretical point of view, the division is necessary in order to apply the concept of marginal utility—that is, the increase in benefits associated with an increase in one or more of the factors upon which the benefit is dependent. For example, what benefit would result from adding $100,000 to the library budget as opposed to the counseling center or any number of alternatives? In the world of the business firm, the best investment of incremental or marginal resources is that which maximizes returns or benefits. In many resource allocation situations, conditions of diminishing marginal utility may act so as to increase, yet not maximize, total utility or returns. Incremental or marginal analysis therefore becomes the key to assessing and maximizing total benefits.

Past allocation strategies based explicitly on this model include zero-based budgeting (ZBB) and the benefit-cost component of PPBS. Zero-based budgeting seems to have faded from the scene, but benefit-cost analysis continues as an important decision calculus. More recently, performance budgeting and decision support systems (DSS) have emerged as new variations on this basic model. Performance budgeting, as exemplified in the Tennessee case (Pickens, 1982), allocates incremental funds on the basis of performance ratings on selected indicators of results. One could argue that this approach fits equally well under some forms of incentive planning in the market interaction model, particularly if base rather than incremental funds were allocated in this manner. The DSS approach is similarly not a clean fit because it is more of a tool or technique that, in turn, facilitates the development of an investment model (Lusk, 1982).

The focus of the investment approach is the objective evaluation of anticipated results. There is a heavy information requirement associated with this model, and the approach has come under fire for the difficulty of establishing valid criteria and developing reliable and cost-effective output measures. In addition, some advocates of the goal model are critical of ZBB-type strategies for their ad hoc (as opposed to comprehensive) planning base (Anthony, 1977).

Cost Reimbursement. A third model flowing from the notion that resources can be allocated on the basis of rational calculations is cost reimbursement or formula budgeting. Ideally, a budget formula is a rational calculation of funding needs based upon standards of the cost of doing business. The formula simplifies, objectifies, and routinizes what otherwise might be bitter and irrational political struggles. One can make the case that, in fact, formulas are the results of interest-group bargaining and therefore only stabilize and quantify the results of that bargaining process. But the basic intent of formula budgeting is rational calculation.

Formula budgeting generally relates work activities to the cost of performing these activities. Its origins lie in the move toward greater efficiency or what Schick (1966) called the management movement in budgeting. Touted by presidential commissions for public budgeting in 1912, 1949, and 1955, this strategy was developing simultaneously in higher education. John Dale Russell's work in developing budgetary ratios for various activities was very influential in the trend toward the use of budgetary formulas in many states as a means of resource allocation among institutions. These formulas were used primarily at the state level, although many institutions have used them for internal allocations as well (Meisinger, 1976).

As in the case of health care cost reimbursement strategies (Morgan, 1983), higher education's average cost reimbursement formulas have come under greater scrutiny during the leaner years of the 1970s and 1980s. Hence we have witnessed attempts to develop more "accurate" formulas such as those based on marginal costing (Indiana), or such as the "fixed-and-variable cost" formulas (Wisconsin and Florida).

The simple, average-cost formulas of the past, which covered a wide range of activities under one general formula, were somewhat sloppy, but they allowed institutions the flexibility to fund costs not explicitly recognized in formula factors—for example, equipment replacement and new program development costs or seed money (Enarson, 1979). Moving from the simple but sloppy mode of average-cost formulas to the more accurate yet complex approaches being tried today has its political costs—namely, the difficulty of obtaining widespread understanding and acceptance.

Besides these weaknesses, formulas also tend to perpetuate the past or status quo, principally because they rely heavily on past cost patterns and weightings. A closely related weakness is that innovative or nonincremental planning tends to be driven out by linear-extension planning that uses either the average or the marginal costs of the past.

Market Interaction. The premise that widely dispersed decision makers, presumably closer and more responsive to local conditions and opportunities, can make better resource allocation decisions is a product of both economic and political theory. Adam Smith saw himself as a radical critic of the merchantilist doctrine that justified a variety of state interventions in the economic life of eighteenth-century England, and thus Smith advocated a system that decentralized decision making to market interactions and the "hidden hand" of the marketplace. The political equivalent of market decision making is perhaps best articulated by James Madison in his espousal of dispersing governmental powers and providing for a system of checks and balances. Dispersing power is not only a guard against centralized governmental tyranny but is also the basis for a system of defining the public interest through competing interest groups. Like its economic market counterpart, the political market, if left to work its natural and pure competitive advantages, would produce the most desirable results—that is, results that are desirable for the most people.

Interest-Group Bargaining. In contrast to the highly rational view of resource allocation taken by those espousing rational calculation models, this political view of the policy process connotes images of "smoke-filled rooms," wheeling and dealing, and other behavior that should be eschewed. Popular images aside, an interest-group bargaining model of decision making assumes a highly competitive environment among and within organizations. The process of competing for resources, real or symbolic, and the determination of who secures those resources are at the core of this model (Wildavsky, 1973). The model has evolved out of the political science literature (Truman, 1951) that has focused on how power structures based on interest groups arise, are sustained, and exercise influence; from business literature that has revealed the competitive, coalitional nature of what we might otherwise think to be highly rationalistic organizations (March, 1962; Cyert and March, 1963); from sociological studies of organizations (Bacharach and Lawler, 1980); and from the literature of higher education (Baldridge, 1971; Pfeffner and Salancik, 1974).

This model suggests that resource allocation among or within institutions of higher education is highly subjective and highly political; that interest groups and coalitions of interest groups are the important unit of analysis; and that the resolution of conflict through bargaining and other forms of mutual adjustment are the key processes. The strength of this approach is said to be in its focus on the realm of the feasible and in its attempt to preserve political satisfaction with the outcomes or what Diesing (1962) calls "political rationality."

The weakness of this model lies principally in its tendency to protect the status quo and the interest groups who benefit from the current distribution of resources. Other weaknesses frequently cited, such as the nondirectional course being taken, go to the core of the controversy between advocates of free market as opposed to guided or planned approaches.

Structuring Incentives. This second variation on market interaction is the more purely economic market model, dealing with the organization or structure of the market for particular goods and services. Richard Nelson (1977) refers to this model as the "organizational perspective" in policy analysis. From this perspective, the questions change from "Should the government spend x million dollars on health care?" to "How can we get patients and doctors to consider costs more seriously in making medical decisions?"

The difference between these two questions is substantive; the whole model of analysis is changed from benefit-cost calculations to prediction of human and organizational behavior under various structural changes in organization and incentives. Proposals for health maintenance organizations (HMOs), for example, attempt to change the structure of choice for health care providers, just as proposals for voucher systems attempt to change the structure of choice for the "consumers" of education.

Strategies based on this model focus on incentives and the free play of market forces. Incentives are, of course, present in each model, as those who have worked with budgetary formulas know well. As experience in the health care sector demonstrates, the cost reimbursement approach needs to be carefully integrated with the structuring of incentives. The difference between the two approaches lies more in the free play of or neutrality given incentives under market assumptions as opposed to the more centrally directed approach of formula budgeting.

The classic structuring-of-incentives model in higher education resource allocation was James Conant's "every tub has its own bottom" approach at Harvard. A more contemporary version, and one that has received widespread publicity among the higher education community, is the decentralized planning or responsibility budgeting at the University of Pennsylvania (Zemsky and others, 1978). Zemsky rejects the rational calculation assumption that today's plans can anticipate tomorrow's problems in a world of rapid change: "Technical models, budgetary projections, anticipated income and expense flows, for all their technical refinements, never capture the sense of flux and change that characterizes educational financing" (p. 229).

Asserting that the university has grown too complex for effective centralized control, Zemsky argues that central administrators tend to delay decisions in order to keep their options open as long as possible and to await promised "better information" that will clarify the matter. The alternative budgetary strategy adopted at the University of Pennsylvania is essentially that of "every tub has its own bottom"; each school is free to launch new programs within the limitations of its own income and expenditures. The goals of the strategy are to force a reconciliation of aspirations and income and to place the control of costs at the operating level.

Before tinkering with the incentive structure of an institution, one must have a knowledge of the existing incentive structure. Fenker (1977) has developed a formal evaluation system, but most institutions rely upon more informal means, principally the experience of their administrators in having come up through the ranks.

There are basically two schools of thought among market-oriented budget strategists, somewhat parallel to the deists and theists among theologians. The deists or pure market theoreticians opt for neutrality on the part of the central administration, regents or coordinating board, and legislature. The role of these central bodies is to let competition run, once the game is structured fairly. The theists, on the other hand, see more of an interventionist role for central administration. The legislature, for example, might attempt to induce institutional resource reallocation to meet shifts in student demand by providing fiscal incentives in their budget allocations in such a way as to reward those institutions that comply (Jones, 1978).

Hoenack's (Hoenack and Berg, 1980) notion of "overall" (as opposed to "specific") incentives is a useful perspective on these two schools of thought. Under a system of overall incentives, a school or college operates flexibly under the general objectives of an institution but is held responsible for its outputs and resources. Specific incentives, on the other hand, pertain to a particular issue, such as the extent to which institutions reallocate to meet new enrollment demands. Specific incentive strategies can be quite directive, and, if a budget allocation strategy employs too many specific incentives, they become a means of implementing a rational calculation model (such as goals) rather than a free play of market forces.

The strengths of the structured-incentives model are those cited by Zemsky (Zemsky and others, 1978) and Hoenack (Hoenack and Berg, 1980)—placing responsibility and control at a level where spontaneous and more responsive planning can occur, and providing operating units positive incentives to husband their resources. The weaknesses are in part the classical weaknesses of any market system—namely, that pure market conditions seldom exist. An economic market, for example, is based on (1) establishing a price system for all goods and services, (2) units having control over the factors of production that allow them to respond to market signals, (3) consumers and producers having access to information that may affect their decisions, and (4) the absence of monopolistic elements that distort pricing or improperly influence resource allocation. Hoenack notes that the market model in higher education has only been implemented at private institutions.

Discussion

Current discussions about changing strategies for resource allocation often center around issues of resource reallocation or coping with declining resources. Are the models suggested here equally relevant under these conditions? Do some models seem more appropriate than others under these conditions? New strategies also raise questions, at least to some, about adequate control over public funds. The term most often employed is "accountability" rather than control, but more often than not the intent is the same. Which models offer what kinds of control?

Reallocation of Resources. The literature on resource reallocation and on responses to declining resources suggests a movement towards rational calculation models. In both the descriptive cases reported and the normative models proposed, increased emphasis on strategies that employ centrally determined choice and a rational calculus is noted or prescribed.

The recent experience of Britain's University Grants Committee (UGC) is a case in point and one that is held by some as a model of "successful" rational reallocation under conditions of decline. Faced with major government funding cuts in 1981, the UGC, which allocates funds to Britain's forty-one universities, announced a selective pattern of reductions based on program strengths and on a desired national distribution pattern of degree programs. These closely held, highly centralized decisions on very selective and differential cuts stand in striking contrast to most other cases where across-the-board, short-term survival strategies have been employed (Berdahl, 1982; Morgan, 1982).

Reallocation strategies also tend to confirm the importance of political models that attach more weight to external pressures in effecting change (Pfeffner and Salancik, 1978). Institutional response to these external pressures is most commonly characterized by efficiency measures and a greater interest in investment models, which look for lower-cost ways of achieving comparable benefit levels. Once most of the readily identifiable slack has been wrung out of the system, however, a second stage of strategies seems to emerge, namely the serious mobilization of political defenses. The interest-group bargaining model emerges here in what Cameron (1983) calls the "domain defense" strategy. If external fiscal pressures persist or if the long-term stability of the organization's market appears questionable (as in the case of the enrollment picture for some institutions), then strategic planning models and mission reviews (Caruthers and Lott, 1981) gain increased attention. Expanding existing markets and creating new markets also become the focus of attention as institutions adopt what Cameron terms "domain offense" and "domain creation" strategies.

As previously indicated, conditions of substantial and sustained fiscal uncertainty or fiscal constraint tend to concentrate decisions at the apex of the hierarchy and to employ rational calculations as a basis for decisions. An alternative but less frequently observed response is to push these decisions and calculations down the system or organization, thereby moving more toward market interaction as a decision model. The University of Pennsylvania is an example of an institution faced with fiscal constraints that has pushed the problem of choice out to its various schools and colleges. Deans can then presumably opt for the same variety of models, ranging from a central determination of goals at the college level to a market system of quasi-autonomous departments.

The resource allocation models discussed in this chapter do seem relevant to conditions of fiscal decline and reallocation primarily because they are, fundamentally, decision models applicable to a variety of environmental conditions. Moreover, their relevance is confirmed by various descriptive case studies of institutions under these conditions. The standard or norm held out in most of the literature on this topic is that of rational calculation and, more specifically, either the goal or investment model. This appears to be the case at both system and institutional levels. Market interaction assumptions tend to be less prevalent. The interest group bargaining model is seen paradoxically as both facilitating and inhibiting of change. Interest groups external to the organization, as Pfeffer and others have demonstrated, exercise significant influence on internal organizational changes. Entrenched internal interest groups, on the other hand, are frequently cited sources inhibiting resource allocation reforms in organizations. More radical economic market models, such as the push for deregulation and survival of the fittest found elsewhere in the economy now, are less commonly advocated for higher education.

Control. Wildavsky (1979) notes that critics of market interaction models find some aspects of Adam Smith's "hidden hand" of the market unappealing: (1) its motivation of selfishness; (2) its irrationality; (3) its passivity in accepting results rather than moving decisively ahead; and (4) its unpredictability in the sense of "whatever the future brings is our fate." Will the aggregate of diverse market decisions lead us toward ends that are in the "public interest"? We seem willing to answer this question in the affirmative with respect to our market economy in this country but unwilling, or at least uncomfortable, to answer similarly with respect to public sector resource allocation choices.

Kotler and Murphy's (1981) use of strategic plans as a standard of control fulfills a need that most of us seem to have for a sense of direction and for someone being in charge. In this sense, market interaction models are clearly less attractive.

Market interaction and incentive approaches in the public sector therefore face attitudinal barriers about the sufficiency of controls and theoretical barriers in the nonmarket nature of the public higher education system. The attitudinal barriers are epitomized in a comment made to the author by a former state education official in California, "Sacramento doesn't like incentives." The dislike in this case stemmed primarily from a sense of lack of control. The theoretical barriers lie in the fact that public institutions do not rely principally upon market prices, namely tuition charges, nor do most of them have the flexibility to retain "profits" with their accompanying incentives. These barriers are not insurmountable, however. Budgets in public institutions could be allocated primarily on the basis of student enrollments, thereby simulating tuition income by school or college. Similarly, legislatures could enact statutes allowing institutions to retain year-end balances (this has been done in Utah, for example). The changes are possible, but are they perceived as desirable?

Conclusions

The value of looking at root assumptions and the models that spring from them is that they allow us to understand better the strengths and weaknesses of various proposed strategies. Budgetary innovations come at us in rapid succession, and most administrators sense a need for a framework against which they can assess these innovations.

One concluding point is to be wary of strategies narrowly based. That is, a strategy based solely on the deductive goal model with little provision for market feedback and adjustments depends too heavily on the clairvoyance of the goal formulators and on the knowledge necessary to deduce workable strategies from desired ends. Similarly, market models that rest heavily on assumptions of pure market conditions in all likelihood will soon be abandoned as the imperfections of the market give rise to interest-group dissatisfaction.

Therefore, strategies that are more broadly based and draw upon the selective strengths of various approaches may offer brighter prospects for success. The "policy analysis" movement is a case in point. In the 1970s, policy analysis emerged as the compromise between the PPBS rationalists and the defenders of interest-group bargaining. Policy analysis became the art or science (take your pick) of the possible; it combined an analysis of objectives and alternatives with an assessment of available resources and of the organizational obstacles that might be encountered in implementation. The title of Aaron Wildavsky's (1979) work on this middle ground characterizes the movement—*Speaking Truth to Power: The Art and Craft of Policy Analysis.*

A second concluding point is that successful strategic planning, which appears to be the most pervasive new strategy at this time, seems to this author to be dependent upon: (1) a very perceptive, and perhaps lucky, leader; (2) individuals at the top who do not have their egos and careers tied to objectives initially set; and (3) a system for monitoring and assessing the environment continuously. Keller's (1983) approach to strategic planning recognizes these and other important factors in a broadly based strategic planning model.

If strategic planning is in fact continuous adaptation to changing environmental conditions, then it begins to look more and more like the ad hoc, short-range decision-making characteristic of incremental budgeting and interest-group bargaining models. As Wildavsky (1973) has noted, "When planning is placed in the context of continuous adjustment, it becomes hard to distinguish from any other process of decision" (p. 133).

A final point is that "new strategies" for resource allocation are often criticized as transitory fads that consume the time and limited attention span of hard-pressed administrators. Certainly there is validity to the criticism. But there is also a silver lining. Even though burdensome reforms such as PPBS and ZBB have been largely discarded along with the reams of paper they generated, elements of these strategies have remained and have had a profound influence on resource allocation decisions. Analysis permeates these decisions now; analysis is legitimate and it is expected. There will always be those who lean toward tempering quantitative evidence with judgment and those who favor tempering judgments with quantitative evidence. Each view is legitimate; we can only hope to move toward an appropriate balance.

References

Anthony, R. N. "Zero-Based Budgeting Is a Fraud." *Wall Street Journal*, April 27, 1977.

Bacharach, S. B., and Lawler, E. J. *Power and Politics in Organizations: The Social Psychology of Conflict, Conditions, and Bargaining*. San Francisco: Jossey-Bass, 1980.

Baldridge, J. V. *Power and Conflict in the University*. New York: Wiley, 1971.

Berdahl, R. "Great Britain: Cutting the Budget, Resetting the Priorities." *Change*, 1982, *14*, 38-43.

Braybrooke, D., and Lindblom, C. E. *A Strategy of Decision: Policy Evaluation as a Social Process*. New York: Free Press, 1963.

Cameron, K. "Strategic Responses to Conditions of Decline: Higher Education and the Private Sector." *Journal of Higher Education*, 1983, *54*, 359-380.

Caruthers, J. K., and Lott, G. B. *Mission Review: Foundation for Strategic Planning*. Boulder, Colo.: National Center for Higher Education Management Systems, 1981.

Cohen, M. D., and March, J. G. *Leadership and Ambiguity: The American College President*. New York: McGraw-Hill, 1974.

Cyert, R. M., and March, J. G. *A Behavioral Theory of the Firm*. Englewood Cliffs, N.J.: Prentice-Hall, 1963.

Diesing, P. *Reason in Society*. Urbana: University of Illinois Press, 1962.

Enarson, H. L. "The Uses and Abuses of Cost Information." In R. H. Allen and J. R. Topping (Eds.), *Cost Information and Formula Funding: New Approaches*. Boulder, Colo.: National Center for Higher Education Management Systems, 1979.

Fenker, R. M. "The Incentive Structure of a University." *Journal of Higher Education*, 1977, *48*, 453-471.

Freeman, T., and Simpson, W. A. "Using Institutional Data to Plan Academic Programs—A Case History." In R. B. Heydinger (Ed.), *Academic Program Planning for the 1980s*. New Directions for Institutional Research, no. 28. San Francisco: Jossey-Bass, 1980.

Hoenack, S. A., and Berg, D. J. "The Roles of Incentives in Academic Planning." In R. B. Heydinger (Ed.) *Academic Program Planning for the 1980s*. New Directions for Institutional Research, no. 28. San Francisco: Jossey-Bass, 1980.

Jones, L. R. "Fiscal Strategies to Stimulate Instructional Innovation and Change." *Journal of Higher Education*, 1978, *49*, 588-607.

Keller, G. *Academic Strategy: The Management Revolution in American Higher Education*. Baltimore: Johns Hopkins University Press, 1983.

Key, V. O., Jr., "The Lack of a Budgetary Theory," *American Political Science Review*, 1940, *34*, 1137-1144.

Kotler, P., and Murphy, P. E. "Strategic Planning for Higher Education." *Journal of Higher Education*, 1981, *52*, 470-489.

Lewis, V. B. "Toward a Theory of Budgeting." *Public Administration Review,* 1952, *12,* 42-54.

Lindblom, C. E. *Politics and Markets.* New York: Basic Books, 1977.

Lusk, E. J. "Decision Support Systems: The Next Research/Practice Connection." *Human Systems Management,* 1982, *3,* 54-55.

March, J. G. "The Business Firm as a Political Coalition." *Journal of Politics,* 1962, *24,* 662-678.

March, J. G., and Olsen, J. P. *Ambiguity and Choice in Organizations.* Bergen, Norway: University Press, 1976.

Meisinger, R. J., Jr. *State Budgeting for Higher Education: The Uses of Formulas.* Berkeley: Center for Research and Development in Higher Education, University of California, 1976.

Morgan, A. W. "Resource Allocation Reforms: Marginal Utility Analysis and Zero-Based Budgeting in Higher Education." *Higher Education Review,* 1977-1978, *1,* 1-17.

Morgan, A. W. "College and University Planning in an Era of Contraction." *Higher Education,* 1982, *11,* 553-566.

Morgan, A. W. "Cost as a Policy Issue: Lessons from The Health Care Sector." *Journal of Higher Education,* 1983, *54,* 279-293.

Nelson, R. R. *The Moon and the Ghetto.* The Fels Lectures on Public Policy Analysis. New York: Norton, 1977.

Pfeffner, J., and Salancik, G. R. "Organizational Decision Making as a Political Process: The Case of a University Budget." *Administrative Science Quarterly,* 1974, *19,* 135-151.

Pfeffner, J., and Salancik, G. R. *The External Control of Organization: A Resource Dependence Perspective.* New York: Harper & Row, 1978.

Pickens, W. H. "Performance Funding in Higher Education: Panacea or Peril?" Paper presented at the 8th Annual Conference on Higher Education, Tucson, Arizona, December 1982.

Schick, A. "The Road to PPB: The Stages of Budget Reform." *Public Administration Review,* 1966, *26,* 243-258.

Truman, D. B. *The Governmental Process: Political Interests and Public Opinion.* New York: Knopf, 1951.

Wildavsky, A. "If Planning Is Everything, Maybe It's Nothing." *Policy Sciences,* 1973, *4,* 127-153.

Wildavsky, A. *The Politics of the Budgetary Process.* (3rd Ed.) Boston: Little, Brown, 1974.

Wildavsky, A. *Speaking Truth to Power: The Art and Craft of Policy Analysis.* Boston: Little, Brown, 1979.

Zemsky, R., Porter, R., and Oedel, L. P. "Decentralized Planning: To Share Responsibility." *Educational Record,* 1978, *59,* 229-253.

Anthony W. Morgan is executive assistant to the president at the University of Utah.

Formula budgeting strategies continue to evolve in response to old weaknesses, changing conditions, and new priorities.

Formula Budgeting: The Fourth Decade

Paul T. Brinkman

Formulas, or mathematical statements that link state appropriations to institutional characteristics (such as work load, costs, output, and so on), are used as part of the funding process for public higher education in roughly half of the states. The number of these states changes over time, as do the formulas themselves and the ways in which they are used. Yet formula budgeting remains one of the most important and widespread funding mechanisms. The focus of this chapter is on ways in which formulas are being changed: why, how, and by whom. Ways of thinking about and categorizing the new strategies reflected in those changes are presented, and future prospects are discussed.

An analysis of formula budgets is complicated by the fact that these budgets continue to evolve even while being analyzed. The problem is especially acute if we want to locate an example of a particular development in a given state. Some states review their formula (or formulas) annually, but the occasional minor adjustment between annual reviews seems to be the rule rather than the exception. Thus, this chapter puts more emphasis on conceptual analysis than on newslike reporting of who is doing what at a particular moment. At the same time, illustrations of current behavior will be used for the sake of concreteness, even at the risk of early obsolescence.

Why is it necessary (at least occasionally) to change formulas? The detailed response to this question is part of the body of this chapter. Here we can note that there are several basic reasons why formulas change: (1) The reality within which formulas must function is constantly changing. Both the objective dimension (largely the demographics and economic conditions) and the subjective dimension (the attitudes, expectations, and goals of the many persons with a stake in the higher education enterprise) are in constant flux. (2) Insofar as formulas represent institutional characteristics such as work load and costs, they are always only approximations. In effect, formulas are models, and, like all models, at any given time they capture only a portion of reality. Thus there is always the possibility that they could be made to represent reality better. What was once a good, or useful, formula may now be dangerously out of step; formulas must change just to stay even. (3) Formulas change because so much depends on them. They serve as guidelines for the transfer and distribution of hundreds of millions of dollars. Often even a slight change in a formula will have profound effects on the amount or the pattern of revenue allocation. In short, formulas change because they are worth changing.

In the sections that follow, we begin by sketching the historical development of formulas, pondering the meaning of "formula," and analyzing what are said to be the strengths and weaknesses of formulas. The particular pressure points for change during the past few years are then considered. All of this forms a basis for discussing the new formula budgeting strategies that have been implemented, or at least considered, recently. The chapter concludes with a section on the implications of these new strategies for institutional researchers and data analysis.

Background on Formulas

The use of formulas goes back to 1951, when four states (California, Indiana, Oklahoma, and Texas) were developing or had incorporated the formula approach in some fashion. By 1963, only six states were using formulas, but by 1967, the number had jumped to sixteen (Gross, 1979). The number continued to increase during the next several years, reaching a total of twenty-five in 1973, but it has remained roughly constant since then. A 1977 study by the Kentucky Council on Higher Education reported a figure of twenty-two states, while in 1982, twenty-six states indicated that their appropriations were largely formula-based, with three more reporting limited use of formulas (Leslie, 1983). As McKeown (1982) notes, not only does the total change but also the composition by state changes as states develop, abandon, and return to formula budgeting.

A complicating factor in obtaining accurate and consistent counts is the ambiguity in the definition of "formula" and the considerable range in the extent to which a formula can be applied and can be influential in the budgeting and funding process. In any event, the conventional wisdom that formula budgeting is a significant factor in about half of the states seems about right.

Definition. Starting with Miller (1964), a number of authors have sought to clarify the nature of a formula budget. This ongoing clarification process has produced a series of definitions that highlight different aspects of formulas. Consider the following selection: an objective procedure for estimating the further budgetary requirements of a college or university (Miller, 1964); subjective judgments expressed in mathematical terms (Meisinger, 1975); a combination of technical judgments and political agreements (Meisinger, 1975); policy judgments in quantitative terms (Jones, forthcoming); and a mathematical means of relating the work load of a public institution to its state appropriation (Pickens, 1981).

Can it be that a formula budget is all of the above? Yes, if one is willing to view formulas from a variety of perspectives. The objective procedures are ways of handling, relating, and implementing subjective judgments, once those latter judgments are expressed in mathematical (that is, quantitative) terms. Technical judgments are present in most formulas, but few such judgments are either purely technical or sufficient in themselves. For instance, some formulas are based on historical cost analyses that essentially are technical appraisals. Yet most who are familiar with costing in higher education would agree that costing is as much art as it is science. And when the ground shifts from what costs have been to what they will be or should be—a shift that is inevitable in any use of formula budgets—then the inadequacy of a purely technical approach is made clear and the need for political negotiation becomes obvious.

Similarly, policy judgments are unavoidable in formulas: How will graduate instruction be funded relative to undergraduate instruction? Will extension courses be funded? Will faculty salaries move with salaries at peer institutions? The list can be a long one, and the decision about what is included among the policy judgments to be manifested in the formula is itself a matter of policy. And, finally, the basic intent of most formulas is to relate work load to appropriations, however objectively, subjectively, technically, or politically that work load may be determined. In the end, a formula budget is a *standard* as much as an *instrument* for resource allocation.

The role of formulas and some of the consequences of their use are further illuminated when formulas are understood as the centerpieces of *bureaucratic* decision-making processes. All states, whatever their funding mechanism, are faced with the basic requirement of allocating state resources to support higher education on an annual (in a few cases, biennial) cycle, and the same basic factors—level of state revenues, student demand/institutional work load, institutional "productivity," prices of resources and purchased services, and so on—are in one way or another factored into the final decision. As Jones (forthcoming) emphasizes, it is the *process* surrounding that decision that helps to distinguish formula approaches to budgeting from other approaches. Once established, formulas can routinize, and to some extent, depoliticize the decision process, and can reduce that process to the implementation of agreed-upon procedures.

It must also be said, however, that the role formulas actually play at any given time varies greatly from state to state. Gross (1979) captures part of this phenomenon by emphasizing the distinction between formulas used to allocate funds and formulas used to request funds. Equally significant is the fact that in some states formulas are critically important in the funding process, while in other states formulas are more a matter of ritual than of substance and are largely ignored when funding decisions are made. McKeown's (1982) use of the term "guidelines" to refer to formulas connotes a kind of middle ground between those extremes, one that probably contains the majority of formulas. In any case, formula-use issues in this sense are beyond the scope of the present discussion, but they should be kept in mind when considering various formula budgeting strategies.

Criteria for Evaluating Formulas. With this view of the multifaceted nature of formula budgets in mind, we cannot be surprised that they have been judged along multiple dimensions. This is certainly true for the evaluative criteria that have been developed; those criteria that formulas are supposed to meet if they are to be good, proper, useful, legitimate, and so on. Some of the proposed criteria relate to what might be called "technical correctness," based on the presumption that formulas are essentially representations, or models, of institutional reality (costs and work load in particular). To be technically right, a formula should: recognize the varying costs of instruction related to disciplines and levels of programs (Gross, 1973); only contain factors that are quantitatively definable (Halstead, 1974); facilitate comparisons with other institutions within and outside of the system (Halstead, 1974); recognize the diverse financial needs of institutions (Miller, 1964); be broad-based, recognizing needs in various functional areas, not just instruction (Gross, 1973); employ methodologies chosen on the basis of their appropriateness to the specific activities to be funded (Miller, 1964); and be able to treat equitably institutions of varying enrollment levels and of varying degrees of maturity (Greene, 1970).

Other proposed evaluative criteria for formula budgets refer more to basic values, arguing that formulas should improve or maintain equitable treatment among participating institutions (Gross, 1973), involve a relationship to standards of quality (Summers, 1975), support the statewide incentive structure (Stumph, 1970), not be used for budget control but be applicable only to budget requests or appropriations rather than internal allocations (Miller, 1964), and preserve institutional management flexibility to the maximum extent possible (McClintock, 1980).

Finally, there are evaluative criteria for formula budgets that relate to the budgeting process. In order to facilitate that process, formulas should be clear and understandable (Halstead, 1974), be as simple as possible so that they can be presented to laypersons (McClintock, 1980), show some benefits to all the major participants in the budget process (Miller, 1964), be adequate for displaying institutional needs to the legislative and executive branches (Stumph, 1970), and inject objectivity into the budget process (McClintock, 1980).

Taken together, then, the evaluative criteria indicate that a good formula is technically correct, representative of certain basic values, and helpful in making the budgeting process work smoothly. These criteria form the background, by and large, for assessments of what is good and bad about the way in which formulas actually work. For present purposes, it is appropriate to concentrate on the less fortunate aspects of formulas because they are the likely source of change and new strategies; a brief review of the positive side is included so as to balance the presentation.

Strengths. Much of what is said to be good about formula budgeting has to do with the salutary effect of formulas on the budgetary process. Commentators point to the way formulas enhance the uniformity and ease of budget preparation and presentation (Hale and Rawson, 1976); the assistance they provide in making comparisons among institutions, programs, and activities (Moss and Gaither, 1976); the way they promote effective communication between the institutions and state-level budget decision makers (Caruthers and Orwig, 1979); the way they make explicit the factors to be considered in the decision process, thereby directing the focus of attention to a select set of policy variables (Jones, forthcoming), or, as Meisinger (1975) puts it, the way they "establish the areas of discretion and the limits of debate" (p. 7); their routinization of the decision-making process, which helps to minimize conflict between the institutions and state budget makers (Caruthers and Orwig, 1979) and which both saves legislative time and permits more time to be devoted to special issues (Allen, 1980); the way they eliminate "politics" from the decision process once the formula has been established (Jones, forthcoming); and their provision of a reasonably simple and understandable basis for deciding on appropriations (Millett, 1974).

As decision rules, formulas remove uncertainty from the decision process. According to Meisinger (1975) uncertainty is reduced through each of four functions performed by formulas: (1) reducing the complexity of budgetary standards, (2) accommodating different organizations—formulas provide an agreed-upon framework for discussion, (3) establishing the limits for the size of the increment to be added or subtracted from the budget base, and (4) providing an "objective" basis for the determination of institutional "fair shares," the convergence of expectations on roughly how much each institution receives. Others agree that formulas provide a method whereby funds can be equitably distributed among institutions (Hale and Rawson, 1976; Moss and Gaither, 1976; Miller, 1964). Since the budget requests for all institutions are calculated according to the same set of procedures, at least the *process* is equitable; whether the substance within the process is itself equitable is another matter (Jones, forthcoming).

Weaknesses. In considering the weaknesses, or disadvantages, of formula budgets, we will employ here a structure that the reader may have already invoked in weighing the plausibility of the advantages proposed for formulas. The good or bad qualities of formulas may be intrinsic (that is, present irrespective of circumstances) or extrinsic (that is, application-specific: sometimes present, sometimes not). A third category—to be precise, a subcategory of the extrinsic—might be called "tendencies" to represent the qualities that formula budgets will likely have unless some deliberate countermeasures are taken. These latter qualities are of major concern for present purposes, for, logically, they are the prime targets for improvement strategies. Other extrinsic features, truly idiosyncratic in nature, need not detain us.

Among the properties of formula budgets that have been seen as weaknesses, the following would seem to be intrinsic: formulas do not self-adjust for a basic, improper level of funding (University of Wisconsin System, 1982); formulas are ill suited to reflect the nonquantifiable elements of educational activities (Allen, 1980); and formulas cannot make policy decisions, yet they embody policy decisions the ramifications of which are often not foreseen (Miller, 1964).

The very nature of formula budgets would appear to entail these disadvantages—and the problems they create—as the price to be paid for obtaining the benefits of formulas. The problems cannot be eliminated directly, although palliative actions are sometimes possible—for example, taking extra care to be right the first time so that proper rather than improper levels of funding are perpetuated.

A second set of weaknesses, in the form of undesirable tendencies, are likely to be present but can be avoided. These tendencies are often the focus of attention for states that embark on improving their formulas or who wish to adopt the best possible formula at the start. The list of unfortunate tendencies is as follows:

1. Formulas are likely to be based on past behavior. Thus, there is a strong tendency to reduce what should be to what has been. Formulas

end up merely projecting rather than predicting budgetary requirements (Miller, 1964). Adjustments for inflation get at only part of the problem.

2. Formula budgets based on costs tend to be simplistic with regard to underlying cost calculations. While this tendency smooths the budgeting process, it often limits the technical correctness and basic validity of the formula. For instance, a linear approach to the size-cost relationship is simple to execute, but it ignores economies of scale, fixed versus variable costs, and so on, and can cause havoc for institutions experiencing substantive enrollment declines (Boutwell, 1973).

3. Formulas tend to have a "leveling" effect on institutions and their quality (Gross, 1973). As a bureaucratic device, there is good reason that a formula should be kept simple and regular in its application. One way to do that is to treat all institutions alike. If treated alike for a long enough period, however, diverse institutions will become similar. Perhaps not everyone will be equally concerned about the loss of diversity per se; unfortunately, the process is more likely to be a leveling *down* than a leveling *up*.

4. Formula budgets tend to be rigid. They are based heavily on what has been and thus often discourage the development of new and innovative programs and technologies (Hale and Rawson, 1976). In particular, formulas typically fail to recognize and fund nontraditional learning, continuing education activities, and other such efforts to attract older students (Moss and Gaither, 1976).

5. Formula budgets will always contain a reward structure, a set of incentives (implicit or explicit) that encourages certain forms of institutional behavior. There is a tendency for institutions to develop programs and practices that will produce maximum results under the formula (Gross, 1979). Because of the nature of most reward structures to date, institutions are thus likely to end up with more high-cost programs than otherwise would have been the case, or to place undue emphasis on awarding "fundable" credits (Caruthers and Orwig, 1979).

6. While formulas are intrinsically bound up with quantification, there is also a tendency to include only what is *readily* quantifiable. Thus formulas tend to be based primarily, if not solely, on input measures such as enrollment or student credit hours, and they give little attention to performance measures such as change in knowledge or skills (Pickens, 1982). When tied to input measures, the reward structure for institutions tilts heavily in favor of growth in size.

7. Formulas tend to focus on meeting current fiscal needs, with little attention paid to long-range issues, such as deferred maintenance and equipment replacement, and to long-term obligations in the form of pension funds (Pickens, 1981).

8. Formulas tend to be slow in reacting to fluctuations in the prices of commodities (Moss and Gaither, 1976); they are often ineffective in

dealing with differential changes in commodity prices (Pickens, 1982); and they usually fail to recognize new costs imposed by social mandate (Pickens, 1982). In other words, as bureaucratic devices, formulas are often ineffective in dealing with changes imposed from without.

9. While it is not the fault of formula budgets as such, there is a tendency to use formulas as a means of budget control—that is, to use the formula budget (in essence, a requesting device) to exert control over internal allocations and expenditures (Allen, 1980).

It appears, then, that a state can get into a fair amount of difficulty by relying on formula budgeting as the basis for making appropriations to higher education. Furthermore, there has been a series of developments in recent years that has exacerbated several of the problems created by the tendencies just delineated. As we noted earlier, formula budgets first appeared in the 1950s and then became widespread in the 1960s. That era differs from the 1980s in several important respects. First, the late 1950s and the 1960s were years of unprecedented growth in higher education. Formula budgets were one of the mechanisms developed to deal with enrollment growth, and they were quite effective. Had the originators realized fully the extent to which many of the formulas *fostered* growth and not merely *accommodated* it, they might have been a little more careful. In any event, the incentives for growth were in accord with the times, and, as is now widely recognized, the linear approach used in most formulas to estimate resource requirements served the institutions and the consuming public well. This approach made enhancements in quality and program offerings possible by generating "excess" revenues for the institutions. Except for a modest number of states in the South and West, the task of providing for enrollment growth has been replaced in the 1980s by the problem of dealing with stagnant or declining enrollments. The original growth incentives threaten now to result in lower admission standards and questionable recruiting practices.

Second, while resources are always limited, the financial problems experienced by many states during the past several years have been more severe than those experienced during the 1960s. The extended duration of difficult financial times has left a higher education legacy of deferred maintenance, lower faculty salaries (in real terms), and less organizational slack. High-cost programs are less tolerable. Growth in higher education is no longer considered desirable in some states even when possible. The original pattern for formulas contained few, if any, incentives for efficiency and prudent management, little recognition of long-range issues, and little provision for reacting quickly and differentially to changing prices. Those inadequacies have become more critical under current conditions.

Third, the concern for quality in higher education is gradually becoming more urgent. Although recent media attention has been focused on primary and secondary education, higher education has not been invisible given the decline in Scholastic Aptitude Test (SAT) scores, the lack of basic skills on the part of many college graduates, and so on. Along with the general public and the government, institutions are interested because they want to do a good job and because it is becoming much harder to use enrollment growth as a basis for increased revenues. So the old formula pattern, with its emphasis on inputs and its ignoring of quality measures, looks increasingly inadequate. As a recent task force (Task Force on the Future Funding of Post-Secondary Education, 1982) put it: "Lack of incentives may not have adversely affected the quality of postsecondary education in an era of growth. A lack of incentives for quality in an era of contraction, however, could result in an erosion of the quality of postsecondary education" (p. 33).

Finally, even the "leveling" tendency of formula budgets appears to be a more serious weakness. When tight financial times are coupled with a desire to enhance quality, states may find that greater diversity and specialization are the best way to optimize the return on their investment dollars. If so, formulas will have to change to be effective, giving greater recognition to existing or planned institutional differences.

New Strategies

Looked at from a nationwide perspective, the evolution of formulas appears to be quite uneven. The histories of formulas in a few states suggest that, for all their alleged rigidity, formulas are likely to change periodically at least in some limited way (see, for instance, Alabama Commission on Higher Education, 1983; Legislative Finance Committee, 1982; and the historical account of formulas in Texas, California, and Illinois in Meisinger, 1975). On the other hand, the formula in Georgia has gone without substantive change since 1963 (Study Committee on Public Higher Education Finance, 1982). Furthermore, what is new to one state and its approach to formula budgeting may be old in another state. And what looks like the same strategy being used in two or more states may in subtle but important ways be different in practice.

Given the complexities and unevenness of the situation to be described, we will use the following two-step procedure in an attempt to convey an accurate sense of how formulas seem to be evolving. The initial focus will be on the strategies directed toward the problem areas that were discussed in the previous section—enrollment, costing, and the like. The focus will then shift to aspects of the recent and extensive formula revision in Kentucky, and, more briefly, in Minnesota—the purpose being to illustrate how states are combining a variety of strategies when they decide to change course in a major way.

Decoupling. Enrollments in public colleges and universities are either stable or beginning to decline in many states; in others, the enrollments are still growing but often with little revenue to support the growth; and some states have both growing and declining institutions. In any case, a strategy that has become widespread over the past few years is to find ways of loosening linear relationships between enrollment and appropriations. In a fifty-state survey done in late 1982, Leslie (1983) found that that relationship was perceived to be loosening in thirty-one states, many of which use formulas.

A formula-based, linear relationship between enrollment and appropriations can be weakened in essentially two ways: decoupling or buffering. The former simply eliminates the connection altogether for one or more formulas in the set that comprises the funding mechanism. For example, while the request for support in the instructional area may be a function of enrollment, the request for support of the library may be a function of some nonenrollment factors such as program emphasis or level of instruction. This approach is now being used to some extent in most formula budgeting states (Spence and Weathersby, 1981).

Buffering. Buffering is being done in a variety of ways. Tennessee uses what might be called a corridor or threshold approach. Any enrollment change that is no larger than plus or minus 2 percent elicits no change at all in funding; and 2 percent is subtracted from any larger change before the funding request is made (for example, a 6 percent change is treated as if it were only 4 percent). In Florida, the amount that the funding level may change in any given year is restricted to a certain range irrespective of what happens to enrollment. In Pennsylvania, a "hold-harmless" clause allows institutions experiencing enrollment declines to be allocated more funds than they would have been entitled to on the basis of formula calculations.

A few years ago Minnesota instituted an arrangement that the state refers to as "bulge funding." Any additional enrollment beyond 1977 levels is not being funded via appropriations. Nor is there any loss of funding due to enrollment declines so long as enrollment stays above the 1977 level. In other words, in the bulge area there is no connection between changes in enrollment and changes in appropriations.

California buffers the effect of enrollment change in its state university system by aligning certain personnel positions with a step function. For instance, smaller institutions are allowed to have fewer students per dean than are larger institutions in steps established at 1,000, 4,500, and 10,000 full-time equivalent students.

For several years ending in 1981, Ohio buffered by guaranteeing that institutions would receive 96 to 98 percent of the previous year's state subsidy, regardless of enrollment change. In Missouri, buffering is accomplished in the instructional formula by recognizing only 90 percent of the actual percentage change in enrollment for institutions with an enrollment increase. For institutions experiencing a decrease in enrollment, the "marginal adjustment" is 70 percent.

Virginia has established funding floors for its small institutions. Virginia's approach has no impact for an institution above the funding floor, but it does provide for long-term stability in the face of continued enrollment decline. On the other hand, buffering with a corridor, or providing a guarantee that is close to but less than 100 percent of the previous year's level, lends short-term stability but offers no solution, other than a more gradual descent, for a long-term enrollment decline.

Using Head Counts of Students. Another enrollment-related strategy bears mentioning. It does not have to do with loosening the connection between enrollment and appropriations but with altering it so as to reflect a change in the composition of the student body. Enrollment is often expressed in full-time equivalent (FTE) terms, but several states are recognizing the growing impact of part-time students by using headcount figures instead of FTE figures for some portions of the budget, such as student services. Maryland, for instance, provides its community colleges with a small additional sum of money over and above the basic formula amount for each part-time student enrolled.

While it is erroneous to view a formula budget as a model of organizational behavior per se, most formulas model at least a large portion of the aggregate financial needs of an institution within the areas they cover. Chronic and substantive disparity between the formula's estimated needs and the actual needs of an institution undermine acceptance of the formula. In addition to the enrollment-related strategies just discussed, two other broad types of strategies are being used to bring formulas more into line with institutional realities. Costs are being calculated or estimated in alternative ways, and formulas are becoming more complex.

Improving Cost Calculations. Many states have reformed their formula budgets by improving cost analysis (Pickens, 1981). In essence, a formula expresses the prices that the state is willing to pay (and the institutions are willing to accept) for a particular set of services. While costs in higher education are generally thought to be much too soft to *determine* prices (see Bowen, 1980, for an extended discussion of the nature of costs in higher education), many would argue that there must be at least a plausible relationship between costs and prices in order to preserve formula legitimacy as well as to permit institutions to carry out their responsibilities in an acceptable manner. Typically, average cost (total cost divided by the units of service) has been the type of cost used as the basis for formula budgets. The new costing strategies are simply alternative ways of overcoming problems that can occur in using an average-cost approach.

The basic problem, which Gross (1979) refers to as the "linear-behavior syndrome," is not intrinsic to the use of average costs per se. Rather, the problem lies with the assumption that average costs behave in a linear fashion; in other words, the assumption is that average costs will be the same regardless of the scale of operations, and thus that there are neither economies nor diseconomies of scale. Average costs will in fact be nonlinear under two conditions: if marginal costs (the change in total cost that accompanies an additional unit of output) are greater or less than average costs, or if at least some costs are fixed (that is, not related to the level of output).

New strategies have been developed with respect to both possibilities. In California, for example, appropriations for additional students at the community colleges are provided at a rate that is two-thirds that of the average revenue per student in the state. In other words, the assumption is that marginal costs are less than average costs by about one-third. Similarly, if enrollment declines, the marginal savings are assumed to be less than the average cost by about one-third, and appropriations are adjusted accordingly. Note that in this instance the *difference* between marginal and average costs is assumed to be constant—that is, not a function of scale or of the extent or direction of enrollment change between budget cycles.

Although not a formula budgeting state, Indiana uses a formula-like relationship between enrollment change and change in the appropriations request. Marginal costs are assumed to be less than average costs (based on cost studies done in the mid 1970s), but, unlike California, in Indiana the difference is made a function of the extent of enrollment change.

Formula budgets that incorporate explicit differences between marginal and average costs are not widespread, nor are they likely to become so. Marginal costs, unlike average costs, cannot be calculated directly in most instances. Instead, they must be estimated, and available procedures to that end are often unsatisfactory, at least when viewed from the perspective of determining formula rate factors (Allen and Brinkman, 1983). The history of Indiana's attempts to derive acceptable marginal-cost values shows how difficult it is to find convincing empirical evidence for any specific set of values (Allen and Topping, 1979). What seems to be happening instead is that states are choosing decoupling or buffering procedures that, in effect, provide marginal adjustments (in funding levels) to enrollment changes. We can put it another way: A direct marginal-cost approach entails changing the formula rates from average to marginal; the indirect approach to marginal costing leaves the rates as they were but changes the base factor. In buffering, for instance, the actual enrollment figure, which would normally constitute the base, may be replaced by an average (or some previous) enrollment figure, thus dampening the effect of the most recent enrollment change. Decoupling has a similar effect, since the funding response to an enrollment change becomes a composite of a (possibly) linear response for some components plus no response at all for the decoupled components, adding up to a dampened, or marginal, response overall.

A related strategy is the explicit recognition of fixed costs. McKeown (1982) notes that, in a survey of twenty-eight states using formula budgets, thirteen reported the use of a fixed-cost component in one or more of their formulas; of those thirteen, seven recognized fixed costs in the instructional area, seven in the general administrative and physical plant areas, and nine in the library area.

As in the case of using marginal-cost estimates, the problem with fixed and variable costs is not in the concept but in the execution. No one doubts that there are fixed costs in each of the functional areas (instruction, administration, and so on) and therefore that there are economies of scale. But formulas are not comprised of general ideas or perceptions; rather, as mathematical expressions, they must embody precise judgments of the degree to which costs in a given area are fixed. Ultimately those judgments will be political agreements, based in some instances on a considerable analytical effort to understand cost behavior and in other instances on very little analysis. In either case, judgments are likely to differ considerably from state to state. For instance, in Texas, 21 percent of "other departmental expense" is considered to be a fixed cost at large institutions. By contrast, in a detailed model under consideration for some time in Ohio, other departmental expense was judged to be 50 percent fixed. And, while Texas does not recognize fixed costs for the remaining expenses in the instructional area, the Ohio model (Baughman and Young, 1982) proposes that "the proportion of first-section offerings by level is the fixed proportion for compensation" (p. 4).

A much simpler, and more typical, approach is that taken by Alabama and other states in which a given funding level is designated as a base amount. Very small institutions get the base amount; larger institutions get the base amount plus additional funds on a per-student basis. The latter funds may be allocated on the basis of rates that in turn vary with institutional size, as is the case, for example, in the Alabama formula and in Florida's formula for community colleges. In Virginia, separate funding floors have been established for four-year institutions (2,500 students) and for two-year institutions (1,000 students), implying that fixed costs are substantively different in the two sectors. In Louisiana, all institutions receive a base appropriation of approximately $1.3 million in recognition of fixed costs and diseconomies of scale.

Making Formulas More Complex. The above attempts to better align formula budgets with institutional cost experiences deal with only one aspect of the alignment problem—the variation of costs with the scale of operations. The operations themselves are complex and have different cost experiences irrespective of scale. The evidence suggests that formulas are evolving toward greater recognition of those differences as well. According to Pickens (1981), the "clear trend is toward applying a different state formula to each of the (program) classifications or to clusters of them" (p. 2). The phenomenon is widespread. In a 1980 survey, for instance, seventeen states reported using formulas in each of five program areas—instruction, administration, library, student services, and plant operations and maintenance (McKeown, 1982). Not only are numerous areas covered but they may also be addressed by more than one formula. In that same survey, Oregon reported having no less than nineteen distinct formulas. And within particular formulas, there is often differentiation by discipline, levels of enrollment, and type of institution. This is especially true in the instructional area, less so in other areas.

The impetus toward complexity is based on the desire not only to align formula budgets with actual expenditure patterns but also to counter the "leveling" tendencies of formula budgeting. Greater recognition of institutional differences is a straightforward way of preventing, or at least slowing down, the leveling process. For instance, the recent recognition of the research area in Maryland's formula structure, along with greater differentiation by level of program, will help to maintain the distinctiveness of the state's research-university segment. Tennessee distributes funds for research in proportion to the amount of funds raised by the institution from other sources in support of research. This approach serves to reinforce the research mission of institutions that already have research capacity and discourage it elsewhere.

Addressing the Quality Issue with Formulas. A longstanding criticism of formula budgeting is that the approach tends to concentrate on input measures, to the detriment of quality considerations. One of the older and more widely employed strategies to maintain or enhance quality is to fund one (or more) of the institutions in the system, usually referred to as the "flagship" institution, at a higher level than the rest of the institutions in the system. This procedure can be carried out in a formula budget by the use of differential rates (for example, dollars per student, or students per faculty). California and Texas are among the states with a history of using this strategy.

A newer and somewhat more focused strategy for quality enhancement is the so-called programmatic or mission funding approach. It starts with a definition or redefinition of the program or mission of each institution. Then the state attempts a selective, programmatic development of each of its institutions. Florida, with its effort at funding "centers of excellence," is probably the best example of this strategy. Mississippi has also considered the feasibility of establishing centers of excellence in several of its major universities. As Folger (1982) notes, the outlook for this type of approach is not particularly bright because of the political contests it is liable to engender. And, again, the focus tends to remain on input measures.

A related strategy being used by Virginia may generate less political controversy. In its "funds for excellence" approach, all institutions are eligible to compete for limited additional support for excellent programs (or programs with great potential, or that offer a unique service to the state). The approach, which is not part of the Virginia formula, includes provisions for evaluation of achievement levels. By contrast, a Georgia proposal for formula revision contains a recommendation for adding 1 percent to the total budget at each institution in order to support quality improvements (Study Committee on Public Higher Education Finance, 1982). For several years, Florida has employed a separate line-item appropriation for quality improvement. Probably the best-known attempt to develop a mechanism for funding quality improvement has been going on in Tennessee for the past several years. In this "performance funding" approach, up to 2 percent of the budget allocation of each institution is based on a series of performance indicators, such as results on national examinations and accreditation of professional programs.

Thus there is some movement in formula states to address directly the quality issue. Still, as Folger (1982) notes, "the quality of activities is not a direct factor in most funding formulas. Where it is, relatively small portions of the budget (typically 1 to 3 percent) are allocated on quality criteria" (p. 23). Furthermore, the likely trend is toward nonformula categorical grants, rather than toward the integration of funds targeted for quality enhancement within the formulas themselves (Spence and Weathersby, 1981). Perhaps there is a recognition here that the tendency of formulas to work best with input and quantity measures is too strong to try to overcome directly; the more workable approach is to complement a typical formula with another type of funding.

Starting Anew. In 1982, Kentucky began a major effort to review and revise the formulas used in the state for recommending appropriations for its public colleges and universities. A revised formula was subsequently adopted in 1983. The objectives and principles of the review process provide a sense of the current state of formula budgeting.

The objectives were to develop a formula that would: (1) consider institutional needs and statutory, institutional, and geographic missions; (2) provide an adequate level of support for each institution; and (3) distribute funds among institutions in an equitable manner (Kentucky Council on Higher Education, 1983). Perhaps the most striking thing about the objectives is that they sound so familiar. The essential purposes of formulas have not changed, it would seem—at least not at the high level of generality of these objectives.

As more specificity is added, however, we begin to see the nuances that reflect the current situation, rather than that of the 1960s, and that underscore some of the lessons learned in the intervening years. Consider the following formula review principles developed in Kentucky (Kentucky Council on Higher Education, 1983):

1. The review and revision of the formula will be based on the current structure of higher education in the Commonwealth of Kentucky.

2. The formula should be relatively simple but should be capable of reflecting differing institutional needs.

3. There should be common levels of funding of common activities as well as provisions for funding of special activities.

4. The formula will include factors that reflect the differing roles and missions, sizes, locations, and programs of institutions.

5. As many of the formula items as possible should be calculated.

6. Information on comparable institutions and national averages may be used in the formula.

7. The formula will provide a base level of funding for each institution to recognize minimum administrative program needs.

8. The formula should provide management incentives to the institutions to achieve certain desirable goals, such as challenge grants, interinstitutional cooperation, effective management, fund raising, and other similar activities. Disincentives should be avoided.

9. The procedure for requesting state support should include the use of the formula and a mechanism for making special requests (such as for desegregation, computer system costs, renovations and maintenance, joint programs, and new or expanded programs).

10. Special efforts, above and beyond the formula, must be made to assure adequate funding to carry out the commonwealth's and the institution's commitment to desegregation.

11. The formula should provide a buffer against the impact of enrollment fluctuations (p. 8).

Principle one affirms the current structure and, by implication, suggests that growth is not a major concern. Principle two affirms the old virtue of simplicity—but not at the cost of failing to recognize differing institutional needs. Equity is the implied value in principle three, but it is clear that equity is to be distinguished from equality. Principle four is an antileveling pronouncement and is probably the most important of the principles; the Kentucky formula has been referred to as a "mission funding" mechanism. By implication, principle five acknowledges the desirability of having a formula that reflects differences in work-load measures across functional areas.

The use of comparative data in formulas, as acknowledged in principle six, may not be a particularly new strategy, but it is a strategy much in use at the present time. The rates that are used in Kentucky's new formula for the "basic primary mission areas" are in fact based on data from "benchmark" institutions. Using comparative data in this fashion can help to legitimize the formula by countering parochialism and the tendency of formulas to anchor institutions in the past—which may contain both inadequate and inequitable funding levels.

Principle seven acknowledges the phenomenon of fixed and variable costs. In the formula itself, the principle is operationalized in the area of student services, for example, by providing a base level of support for each institution and then generating support for head-count enrollment above the base level for each institution. Note also the use of head-count enrollment, an approach that recognizes both the growing importance of part-time enrollments and the level of work load they tend to create for activities in the student services area.

Principle eight acknowledges by implication the disincentives that have tended to be imbedded in formulas. Also acknowledged is an inclination to grant more management flexibility to the institutions (see Mingle, 1983, for a description of how this is being dealt with in several other states). The principle suggests that formulas in themselves are not necessarily an impediment to institutional management flexibility. Rather, they simply reflect the larger interests of the state at any given time. At the moment, many states are interested in having their institutions make the most of limited resources, raise more money from other sources, and take more responsibility for hard (and sometimes unpopular) choices.

Principle nine recognizes the inherent weakness of formulas as bureaucratic devices in handling special programs, long-term issues, major investments, and innovations. Since these limitations exist, the procedure for requesting state support must include more than the formula. Principle ten makes the same point, but with reference to a particular problem. It would not be fair, however, to assume that only the most standard of programs are dealt with in the new formula. The formula does contain, for instance, provisions for increasing the support level (rate per student) for "preparatory" education, a base level of support for adult and continuing education, and support for summer school.

Lastly, principle eleven acknowledges the difficulties that may be created for institutions by the use of enrollment-driven formulas. In the formula adopted, buffering is accomplished by using a three-year moving-average enrollment as the base for calculations. In addition, institutions are permitted to project enrollment.

It is instructive to note that the Kentucky Council on Higher Education thought it advisable to issue a formal statement of formula-use policy. In it, the Council affirms the need for equity within the system, the need to protect the base budgets of the institutions, and the need to recognize the distinctiveness of each institution. In addition, the Council makes a clear statement (Kentucky Council on Higher Education, 1983) that the formula component for the basic primary mission areas (which comprise the bulk of the funding) is "a system of values to generate state appropriations on an equitable basis; it is not intended to be used for internal budgeting purposes. Each institution should budget internally according to its own priorities" (p. 16).

What distinguishes the Kentucky formula as a contemporary approach to formula budgeting is not so much the inclusion of many new strategies, although there are some—for instance, buffering, fixed-cost components here and there, the integral use of comparative data on out-of-state institutions, and considerable complexity in terms of the areas covered in the formulas. But one does not see much use of esoteric costing techniques or movement toward performance funding. Instead, considerable care has been taken to ensure that the formula addresses the equity issue, maintains institutional diversity and distinctiveness, provides for special and new program needs, and creates useful incentives and flexibility for management.

Looking more briefly at the new formula budgeting approach in Minnesota, we find some commonalities with the Kentucky approach but some interesting differences too. The task force that studied the funding alternatives established the following objectives: provide incentives for innovative resource management, provide resources in an equitable manner, recognize different cost patterns, encourage quality, and encourage productivity (Task Force on the Future Funding of Postsecondary Education, 1982). The commitment to equity and institutional diversity are familiar themes. Creating better management incentives was also a goal shared with the Kentucky task force, but the emphasis on quality and productivity was not. Unfortunately, the formula mechanism that was to operationalize that emphasis was not made a part of Minnesota's new formula. It would have been interesting to see whether *both* quality and productivity could have been enhanced. According to Spence and Weathersby (1981), "the choice in the coming years may have to be between increased productivity and decreased quality of program offerings" (p. 287).

At the heart of the Minnesota formula is a buffered, differential, average-cost funding approach. The buffering is accomplished by relating requested resources to a previous level of full-year equivalent enrollments. The enrollment figures used are those recorded two years prior to the year being funded; for example, 1983 enrollments are used in determining the funding level for 1985. Costs and enrollments are differentiated by program type (twelve categories) and by level of instruction (four categories). With respect to the funding for basic programs, this approach is not much different than Kentucky's, but it should be noted that the cost data are from Minnesota's own institutions while Kentucky incorporates data from benchmark institutions around the nation. The Minnesota task force looked carefully at alternative costing mechanisms, especially program funding, fixed-variable funding, and core funding, but found that average-cost funding met their objectives best—particularly with respect to management incentives. As the task force emphasized, however, theirs is not a pure form of average-cost funding. By tying the average-cost rates to a previous year's level for the base factor (enrollment), the procedure generates changes in the funding request similar, in effect, to those derived on the basis of a direct marginal-costing approach.

There is no provision in the formula itself for funding new programs; the needed resources will have to be added to formula-based levels, a possibility as the state's economy improves, or be created by the institutions themselves through a reallocation process. Minnesota is considering incorporating funding for continuing education, evening courses, and summer sessions within the basic formula. Finally, it should be noted that the new formula will be used for the research university, the system of regional universities, and the community colleges, a move that, at least in a procedural sense, constitutes a considerable shift from previous practices in the state.

Overall Picture. Most of the undesirable tendencies of formula budgets have been countered by one or more of the new strategies. The effects of enrollment changes are being dampened, or marginalized, to protect institutions from decline and (a few) states from further growth. Costing procedures and techniques, which underly many formulas, are getting a bit more sophisticated perhaps, but indirect approaches (for example, conventional average costs plus enrollment averaging) outnumber pure forms. The leveling tendencies of formulas are being countered by greater recognition of institutional differences, as manifested in highly disaggregated approaches to the instructional area, along with the inclusion of, and distinct approaches to, additional functional areas.

The need to incorporate more appropriate incentives for management has been acknowledged and steps are being taken. Finding acceptable ways of funding quality enhancements on a formula basis remains a challenge, but several attempts are being made. There seems to be general acceptance that special programs, innovations, long-term obligations, and capital-intensive projects will continue to be handled best outside of formulas. Recent study groups on funding public education favor using formulas as requesting or allocating devices only, with little inclination toward using them for detailed expenditure control.

The Future. The forces that are driving the new strategies in formula budgeting are not likely to change during the remainder of the decade. Thus it is reasonable to assume that we will witness more of what has been developing in formula budgeting in recent years. Alternatives to pure forms of average costing will continue to be sought. We are likely to see new versions of fixed and variable costing and to find average-cost funding used in conjunction with enrollment buffering to create a marginal-cost effect.

The desire to match funding to real needs and to maintain differences in institutional mission is likely to lead to increased complexity in formulas. Complexity cannot grow indefinitely, though, without undermining the intelligibility of formulas. Furthermore, the cost studies that are required for a realistic portrayal of institutional cost behavior are formidable and expensive. They also carry some risk for the institutions, in that a realistic portrayal of costs provides an attractive basis for greater state control over internal institutional expenditure patterns (Allen and Topping, 1979).

Performance funding has been tried on a very small scale thus far. The impetus seems to be toward more attempts, perhaps on a larger scale. As performance auditing becomes more commonplace, can the link with funding be far behind? Yet definitional and measurement problems remain major obstacles, and political and bureaucratic inertia will militate against moving too far away from the input, activity-level basis that is now so prevalent in formula budgeting.

Incentives for efficient management are likely to appear as attractive options to financially hard-pressed state governments. For the same reason, new formulas are likely to contain incentives for institutions to raise money from other sources—for example, by letting institutions keep the indirect cost reimbursements they receive from outside contractors. Some of these latter incentives are likely to be related to quality enhancement, as in the case where the state matches gifts for endowed chairs.

Implications for Institutional Researchers and Budget Analysts

If the assumption is correct that formula budgeting will continue to develop as it has over the past several years, campus information specialists are likely to play an increasingly important role in the creation, implementation, and evaluation of formulas. There are several reasons why: Formulas are becoming more information intensive, both in terms of their characteristics and the context of their use; the effects of the new strategies, because they are new and often untested, will require detailed evaluation at both state and campus levels; and continuing financial restrictions will keep the margin for error small, which will reinforce the need to understand formula implications.

Any attempt to change a formula so that it more accurately reflects institutional needs is liable to require additional information. It is true that formula rates and the way base factors are constructed and measured are ultimately the product of negotiation; they have to be agreed upon by the parties involved. But as interest increases in matching the agreed-upon values with institutional behavior, more data and information are likely to be needed. For example, if it is decided that the fixed component of institutional costs ought to be recognized, a major analytical effort is likely to be required to operationalize that decision. Baughman and Young (1982) specifically mention the considerable amount of study it took to develop a fixed- and variable-cost model for Ohio. The fact remains that the alternative costing procedures that might be used in place of, or in conjunction with, the traditional average-cost approach, are simple in concept but difficult in practice. This is not to say that a state could not make quick work of implementing one of the alternatives; indeed, there is reason to believe that this has been done in a few instances. But then the goal of making the formula a better model of aggregate need has in fact been given up in favor of purely political ends—an effective solution in the short run perhaps but surely a risky one for the institution's long-term well-being.

Alternative costing schemes are not the only potential cause for data intensification in formula budgeting. The tendency to include more functional areas as separate formula components and the increased disaggregation of elements within an area are also likely to increase the need for data as well as for analysis. For instance, one state is currently thinking of making equipment allocations a separate item in one of their formulas. An institution's allocation for equipment would be an aggregate of the allocation properly due to each of its departments. The objectivity intended by the state will likely require more information than is currently available.

The *nature* of the data and analysis needed in support of formula budgeting may also evolve. If recent movements toward performance funding gain momentum, institutional researchers are likely to find themselves in the middle of new and challenging definitional and measurement problems. Poorly drawn, narrow performance measures could be harmful. Adequately addressing an appropriate range of performance will be a formidable task. Analytical requirements will also be increased if institutions are asked to be more precise about the quality of their assets—faculty and staff, library, equipment, and buildings. Here, much would have to be done to match even the modest standards of objectivity, comparability, and predictability now found in formulas based on inputs and activity levels.

A second major reason why institutional researchers and other institutional data analysts are likely to be important actors as new or revised formulas emerge is that the effects of the new approaches will need to be evaluated and interpreted. Even if the new formula procedures are thought through carefully, it is unlikely that their full impact will be known beforehand. In the critical area of dealing with sustained enrollment declines, for example, there is relatively little experience upon which to draw. We have looked at some of the strategies being devised. Will they work? What unintended results will occur as these strategies are implemented and remain in effect for several years? While numerous individuals may be involved with monitoring the effects at the campus level, we can only hope that institutional researchers, with their campuswide perspectives, will be included in the process.

As the nation's top economists have proven time and again, predicting the health of the economy several years out is difficult. Nonetheless, it is hard to imagine how most state governments could find themselves with a surfeit of resources anytime soon. The basics—the federal budget deficits, the defense buildup, the rising cost of other social services such as medical care, and the deteriorating condition of the nation's physical infrastructure (roads, bridges, dams)—suggest that state budgets will remain under considerable pressure. Thus many public higher education institutions will have to continue operating within fairly tight, demanding financial constraints. Their administrators will need to understand thoroughly the implications of current or proposed formulas both to make their case for adequate funding and to understand the parameters within which they are or will be working.

In the face of what seems to be a growing need to evaluate ever more complex formulas, we can conclude by noting that new data and information processing tools could make the task easier. Readily available microcomputers, for instance, coupled with easy-to-use modeling languages—electronic spread sheets are one type—give institutional researchers and budget analysts an opportunity to examine the effects of various formula options in ways that were difficult, if not impossible, before: Too much time and money were required. With the new technology, it is becoming increasingly possible to play out a variety of "what if" and "how to" scenarios without having to expend an inordinate amount of resources. The insights gained should be helpful in adjusting formula budgets to changing conditions and concerns.

References

Alabama Commission on Higher Education. *Occasional Papers on Higher Education.* Montgomery: Alabama Commission on Higher Education, 1983.

Allen, R. H. *Enrollment Decline and Formula Funding.* Boulder, Colo.: National Center for Higher Education Management Systems, 1980.

Allen, R. H., and Brinkman, P. *Marginal Costing Techniques for Higher Education.* Boulder, Colo.: National Center for Higher Education Management Systems, 1983.

Allen, R. H., and Topping, J. R. *Cost Information and Formula Funding: New Approaches.* Boulder, Colo.: National Center for Higher Education Management Systems, 1979.

Baughman, G. W., and Young, M. E. "A Method for Incorporating Fixed and Variable Costing Concepts in Student-Based Models for State Funding of

Higher Education in Ohio." Paper presented at the Association for Institutional Research Forum, Denver, Colorado, May 17, 1982.
Boutwell, W. K. "Formula Budgeting on the Down Side." In G. Kaludis (Ed.), *Strategies for Budgeting*. New Directions for Higher Education, no. 2, San Francisco: Jossey-Bass, 1973.
Bowen, H. R. *The Costs of Higher Education: How Much Do Colleges and Universities Spend Per Student and How Much Should They Spend?* San Francisco: Jossey-Bass, 1980.
Caruthers, J. K., and Orwig, M. *Budgeting in Higher Education*. ERIC/AAHE Research Report No. 3. Washington, D.C.: American Association for Higher Education, 1979.
Folger, J. "Financing Quality in a Period of Austerity." Paper presented at a meeting of the Southern Regional Education Board, Baltimore, Maryland, June 28, 1982.
Greene, C. "Budget Formulas Help Growing State System Tell Where It's Going." *College and University Business*, 1970, *48*, 58-64.
Gross, F. M. "A Comparative Analysis of the Existing Budget Formulas Used for Justifying Budget Requests or Allocating Funds for the Operating Expenses of State-Supported Colleges and Universities." Monograph No. 9. Knoxville: University of Tennessee Office of Institutional Research, 1973.
Gross, F. M. "Formula Budgeting and the Financing of Public Higher Education: Panacea or Nemesis for the 1980s?" *AIR Professional File*, 1979, *3*, 1-6.
Hale, J. A., and Rawson, T. M. "Developing Statewide Higher Education Funding Formulas for Use in a Limited Growth Environment." *Journal of Education Finance*, 1976, *2*, 16-32.
Halstead, D. K. *Statewide Planning in Higher Education*. Washington, D.C.: Government Printing Office, 1974.
Jones, D. P. *Higher Education Budgeting at the State Level: Formula Funding in Context*. Boulder, Colo.: National Center for Higher Education Management Systems, forthcoming.
Kentucky Council on Higher Education. *Program Funding by Formula of the Unrestricted Current Fund Operation of Kentucky's Public Higher Education Institutions*. Frankfort: Kentucky Council on Higher Education, 1977.
Kentucky Council on Higher Education. *The Final Report of the Formula Steering Committee*. Frankfort: Kentucky Council on Higher Education, 1983.
Legislative Finance Committee. *Final Report of College and University Funding Study*. Helena, Mont.: Legislative Finance Committee, 1982.
Leslie, L. L. "Recent Financing Developments in the Fifty States." In R. A. Wilson (Ed.), *Survival in the 1980s: Quality, Mission, and Financing Options*. Tucson: Center for the Study of Higher Education, University of Arizona, 1983.
McClintock, D. L. *Formula Budgeting: An Approach to Facilities Funding*. Washington, D.C.: Association of Physical Plant Administrators of Universities and Colleges, 1980.
McKeown, M. P. "The Use of Formulas for State Funding of Higher Education." *Journal of Education Finance*, 1982, *7*, 277-300.
Meisinger, R. J., Jr. "The Politics of Formula Budgeting: The Determination of Tolerable Levels of Inequality Through Objective Incrementalism in Public Higher Education." Unpublished doctoral dissertation, University of California, Berkeley, 1975.
Miller, J. L., Jr. *State Budgeting for Higher Education: The Use of Formulas and Cost Analysis*. Michigan Governmental Studies, no. 45. Ann Arbor: University of Michigan Institute of Public Administration, 1964.
Millett, J. D. *The Budget Formula as the Basis for State Appropriations in Sup-*

port of Higher Education. New York: Management Division, Academy for Educational Development, 1974.

Mingle, J. R. (Ed.) *Management Flexibility and State Regulations in Higher Education.* Atlanta: Southern Regional Education Board, 1983.

Moss, C. E., and Gaither, G. H. "Formula Budgeting: Requiem or Renaissance?" *Journal of Higher Education,* 1976, *47* (5), 543-563.

Pickens, W. H. "Statewide Formulas to Support Higher Education." In *Legislator's Guide to Higher Education Issues of the 1980s.* Washington, D.C.: National Conference of State Legislatures, 1981.

Pickens, W. H. "What's Ahead for Higher Education?" *Journal of the National Association of College Auxiliary Services,* April 1982, pp. 8-12.

Spence, D. S., and Weathersby, G. B. "Changing Patterns of State Funding." In J. R. Mingle and Associates (Eds.), *Challenges of Retrenchment: Strategies for Consolidating Programs, Cutting Costs, and Reallocating Resources.* San Francisco: Jossey-Bass, 1981.

Study Committee on Public Higher Education Finance. *Formula for Excellence: Financing Georgia's University System in the '80s.* Atlanta: Office of the Governor, 1982.

Stumph, W. J. "A Comparative Study of Statewide Operating Budget Formulas Administered by Statewide Coordinating Agencies for Higher Education in Selected States." Unpublished doctoral dissertation, Southern Illinois University, 1970.

Summers, F. W. "The Use of Formulae in Resource Allocation." *Library Trends,* 1975, *23,* 631-642.

Task Force on the Future Funding of Postsecondary Education. *Final Report of the Task Force on the Future Funding of Post-Secondary Education.* Minneapolis: Minnesota Higher Education Coordinating Board, 1982.

University of Wisconsin System. *Instructional Funding Report.* Madison: University of Wisconsin System, 1982.

Paul T. Brinkman is a senior associate at the National Center for Higher Education Management Systems, Boulder, Colorado.

*Several examples illustrate the ways in which
incentives may be used in higher education finance.*

New Approaches to Incentive Financing

Richard H. Allen

If it had ever occurred to Mark Twain to think about the use of incentives in higher education finance, he might have delivered himself of the opinion that "no one ever talks about incentive financing but everyone does something about it." Perhaps the reason that the role of incentives in financial decision making is seldom discussed is that there has been little effort to develop a systematic analysis of the financial incentives that operate in higher education and of how they affect educational results.

It seems curious that an underlying principle of our way of organizing activity has received so little attention, yet financial incentives (despite their central place in economic analysis) remained largely unexamined until the rise of organization theory as a body of literature. Financial incentives were simply assumed and used in a one-dimensional way in economic analysis (that is, in profit maximization). Unfortunately, the organization theorists who have so improved the analysis of decision making in general have not, in any significant way, focused on higher education financing mechanisms. Only recently have they focused on higher education at all (Baldridge and others, 1978). The finance analyst can use some of the general precepts of organization theory and can draw on the large literature on public-sector budgeting (which shares many characteristics with practices in higher education), but he or she must usually move in uncharted areas.

With the upsurge in interest in the management of higher education in recent years, numerous claims have been made that the financing system being discussed fosters incentives among the participants in the process. This is not surprising—all systems for transferring resources create financial incentives. This is true from the simplest of financial transactions (for example, "your money or your life") to the very complex (for example, a corporate merger). What is new about some of the innovative financing plans that have been developed in recent years is that they include *explicit* consideration of the incentives involved in a financing scheme and they (sometimes) try to use financial policies to manipulate the incentive structure. While it seems curious that this approach is considered revolutionary, it is a breakthrough compared to its chief rivals for restructuring higher education finance.

In discussing new approaches to incentive financing in higher education, this chapter first looks at five conceptual models of how incentives can operate. We then examine several of the models in practice.

Five Models for Incentive Financing

To understand the role of incentive finance in higher education, we need to focus on the power relationship between the provider of funds and the recipient (in regard to the locus of detailed decision making) and on the various strategies followed by the provider of funds (hereafter known as "the center") to induce specific outcomes. This section presents five models of incentive finance that assume different sets of power relationships and, above all, different strategies that are pursued by the center. While one might define hundreds of different models of incentive finance, the five chosen here cover the entire spectrum of power relationships and strategies and are sufficiently discrete to discuss individually. Obviously, combination models, subvariants, and transitional models are possible, and the overwhelming majority of actual observations will be of these types rather than like the pure models. Nevertheless, the models chosen here do have an analytic value when applied to individual circumstances.

The models to be considered can be arrayed on a two-dimensional scale depending on how centralized the organization is and how explicitly the strategy chosen by the center attempts to issue a set of specified outcomes. The models to be considered are the central-control model, the allocational budget formula model, the outcomes-oriented model, the good-management-practices model, and the full-responsibility model. These five models can be arrayed as follows:

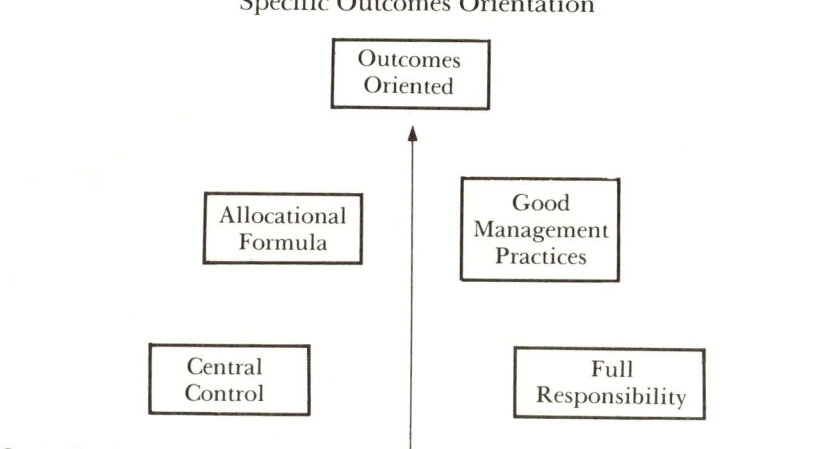

In looking at these models, one might refer to the work of Curry and others (1982) on different models of fiscal relationships between states and institutions of higher education. In one sense, the models here are similar to the models described by Curry and others (1982), but these are more general in their application and are focused on the incentive structure rather than on the organizational arrangement.

Central-Control Model. In both the first and the second model, the incentive structure is not new. This first model is characterized by high levels of centralization and a lack of budgetary focus on specific educational outcomes. The center has sufficient power, either through financial or nonfinancial means, simply to direct that certain activities be performed, certain expenditures be made, and certain results be achieved. In the context of higher education finance, centralized control normally manifests itself through a strong emphasis on budget and accounting control and a focus on objects of expenditure and staff full-time equivalency. Using its power, central administration induces a set of incentives on subordinates. The financial incentives in this model are usually personal ("do this or you will get fired or not receive a pay increase") but may be organizational ("do this or your overall budget will be reduced"). The threat of punishment can be seen as a negative incentive. Specific actions are directed, but the emphasis is on process compliance, not on inducing subunits to pursue overall outcomes. The integration of subunit activities with central priorities is under the control of the central authority.

In its purest Weberian sense (Weber, 1947) of a definite bureaucratic hierarchy with a clear chain of command, this model is seldom, if ever, evident in higher education. Under certain circumstances, however, the model is useful in analyzing the relationship and behavior of two participants in a financial decision. For example, while an academic vice-president may not be able to command and control the faculty, either directly or indirectly, he or she can often command the deans. This does not mean that the vice-president will ultimately achieve institutional purposes but only that the dean does as instructed.

That higher administration, at whatever level, gets its way has a number of advantages. It allows fiscal priorities to be set centrally by those charged with the responsibility. The organization in question theoretically functions as with a single will. Resources can be mobilized to achieve particular goals that are unachievable with only the subunit resources. Formal planning can take place, and resources can be shifted to meet the dictates of the plan. Efficiencies can be achieved by controlling resources centrally; indeed, efficiency is the primary claim of bureaucracy.

As the literature on organization demonstrates, this approach also has significant disadvantages. The central administration can never make decisions at the required level of detail and see that the decisions are carried out. Otherwise, there would be no need for lower levels of administration. A tremendous literature has grown up regarding this locus-of-authority question (for example, Fayol, 1949). When the central administration has the authority to make detailed fiscal decisions, the result will inevitably be decisions that are not fully articulated. For example, a dean may respond to instruction to reduce expenditures by eliminating service courses.

The second major problem for central administration in achieving centralized control, even in a two-party transaction, is that such transactions never exist in an incentive vacuum, even if no incentives are defined by the center. The subordinate party encounters numerous other forces that are not congruent with those induced by central control. Such incentives may come from the subordinates (Hambrick and Mason, 1982), from the subordinates' peers (Roethlisberger and Dickson, 1939), or from a subordinate's counterparts outside the organization (Mintzberg, 1979)—a particularly important group in higher education. All of these factors dilute the power of the incentives induced by central administration and lead to unintended and unpredictable results unless central administration can anticipate and channel the external factors. Finally, the problem of goal displacement plagues this model. When subunits are rewarded for obeying orders, they will do so, often to the exclusion of seeking larger, more important goals (McKeon, 1967).

Allocational Budget Formula Model. In terms of the diagram, this model has a moderate level of central control and some focus on educational outcomes. Allocational budget formulas are based on the funding of certain specified activities or measures of work load performed by the subunits. For example, a state may provide funding to institutions based on the number of student credit hours, the number of students enrolled, the number of academic programs offered, and the number of assignable square feet utilized. All of these measure the work load and, ostensibly, the costs incurred by an institution for such services as instruction, student services, libraries, and the operation and maintenance of the plant.

The incentives generated by allocational budget formulas are similar to, but much less rigid than, those generated by centralized control. Like centralized control, the budget formula will encourage activities that increase the count of things that are to be funded. Thus, it can be expected that institutions will seek to increase their enrollments (generating both student credit hours and head count), will adopt various tuition pricing structures to encourage students to take more credit hours, will engage in program proliferation, will have few constraints on their efforts to obtain capital construction appropriations outside the formula, and will be induced to seek new construction rather than maintain their current physical plant. Since, however, the subunit administrators normally are not constrained to spend resources according to the algorithm that generated them and since the center does not attempt to control detailed decision making, budget formulas are much more flexible than centralized control. For example, funds generated by the head count (supposedly to fund student services) may be spent on physical plant (supposedly funded by the number of assignable square feet at the institution). In this way, the allocational budget formula guards against potential allocational mistakes by the center.

The flexibility in an allocational formula goes farther than prevention of allocational mistakes, however. The subunit leader is free, within the limits of overall resource constraints, to determine the type of services to be performed (at the detailed level) and the mode of service delivery. Thus, one institution may choose to deliver arts and sciences instruction in a lecture/laboratory mode, another may deliver vocational instruction in a scattered-training-site mode. Since no attempt is made to engage in detailed decision making at the center, the most serious problems of centralized control—incomplete decisions and inappropriate locus of control—do not arise.

With this model, it is assumed that the subunits will pursue the outcomes that are the goals of the center but this is by no means certain. Allocational budget formulas provide a great deal of flexibility for subunit leaders but may encourage them to use this flexibility inappropriately to pursue the various funding measures (that is, to engage in goal displacement), or the subunits may pursue inappropriate goals within the constraints of the incentives produced by the formula. These goals may be at odds with the goals of the center and of the institution overall. Formal planning may be difficult under these circumstances.

The previous two approaches to the use of incentives in financing schemes, while very important, can hardly be called new. Both have seen extensive use in higher education for many years. The third, fourth, and fifth approaches, however, are new in the sense that they have not been used widely to date in higher education and they have only recently received attention in the professional literature.

Outcomes-Oriented Model. This model ranks very high on the scale in terms of emphasizing the achievement of specific educational outcomes and is midway on the scale in terms of centralization. In this model, the center determines what outcomes it wishes the subunit to achieve and funds those outcomes directly. Funds are provided on the basis of a formula—so much funding for so much output of a particular type. For example, a state might provide funding based on the number of points an institution's students improve on a standardized test, the number of an institution's graduates finding employment in specified fields within the state, or on the number of refereed journal articles published by the faculty.

No funding is actually provided to cover the costs of the various activities that an institution undertakes in order to accomplish these goals. Funding is only provided upon demonstrated success (as defined in the financing scheme) in achieving the outcomes. The institution is free to use the resources gained from accomplishing the outcomes in any way it chooses. It has a free choice of goals to be pursued (within overall funding constraints) and may seek to achieve the specified outcomes in any fashion (again, within overall funding constraints). Resources may be concentrated on the achievement of particular outcomes or spread across a comprehensive range of outcomes.

Although the mechanics of providing funding based on outcomes are similar to those of allocational formulas, the incentives provided for the subunits are very different. Whereas the allocational formula rewarded the subunit for growing in terms of the activity performed (that is, in terms of its size), the outcomes-oriented approach rewards subunits for producing specified education results. While a larger subunit, all other things being equal, will receive more funding, size alone will ensure little. Indeed, size, in the absence of goal achievement, will merely increase expenditures and hasten the demise of the failing subunit. Without careful attention to phase-in policy and the relative value of different achievements, an outcomes-oriented funding system may induce subunits to concentrate on short-run to the detriment of long-run achievements. For example, subunits might concentrate on annual test scores and neglect faculty scholarship, given the two-year lead time on publication of journal articles. The most dangerous aspect of the outcomes-oriented model is that it provides incentives to accomplish only the specified results—"teaching to the test." Since education is a very poorly understood process, important elements may be left out in setting incentive structures. A set of incentives based on the allocational formula model or on the full-responsibility model is more flexible in allowing the subunits to devote attention to such issues even when the incentive structure does not specifically encourage attention.

Good-Management-Practices Model. This model is moderately decentralized and moderately outcomes oriented. When the center wants to provide incentives to operate according to good management practices, the details of the basic financing system do not matter a great deal. It is only necessary that the funding system provide sufficient discretion to allow subunit managers to employ good management practices. The distinguishing characteristic of this approach is that additional (usually limited) funding is made available to subunits contingent on subunit performance of certain specified administrative, planning, and management research activities. The additional funding may be equal only to the cost of performing the extra activities, or an extra increment may be made available. The theory is that, if the reward for performing the activity at least equals the cost, then the subunits will perform the activity, and the decision-making processes of the subunit will be improved. An inherent assumption, of course, is that better decision making will improve outcomes. Better outcomes are not rewarded; the activities that lead to them are rewarded.

As an illustration, additional funding may be made available for following up students who drop out, transfer, or graduate from a program. Dropouts may return to the program, return to the school in another program, or never return. Transfers may move to other institutions. Graduates may seek further education, work in or out of the field for which they were specifically prepared, or not work at all. Follow-up studies can provide a great deal of information about the relative incidence of each such decision, motives for choices, strengths and weaknesses of various elements of the curricula, insights into admissions and academic advising policy, interactions between instruction and research, and so on. The school is induced by the incentive to perform the study, collect and analyze the information, and make appropriate educational choices to enhance programs.

Full-Responsibility Model. This model is highly decentralized and shows little concern by the center for specific outcomes. In the full-responsibility model, the subunit is responsible for its own actions and its own future. In effect, the subunit is independent except that some or all funding comes from the center. The funding mechanism used is one that simply passes revenue through the center to the subunit as if the subunit were interacting directly with the clientele or constituency. The subunits are part of the center for the purposes of identification in the minds of the public, for performance of overhead functions, and for access to funding sources available only to the center (for example, tax revenue or endowment income). The subunit, within the constraints of its mission and overall funding levels can decide which services it wishes to provide and the method of producing those services. An example of how this system works is the case of a professional school with a special agreement with its parent institution. The professional school receives all the revenue generated by its enrolled students, with an appropriate deduction for logistical services, physical plant services, and the like. The professional school is responsible for hiring and deploying faculty, developing the curriculum, and providing academic support and student services. It is also responsible for its own fiscal position and is not budgeted or controlled (except in a clerical sense) through the parent institution. In short, the professional school is treated largely as if it were free-standing.

The incentive created by such a financing structure is exactly that implied in the title—full responsibility. The subunit can be expected to behave as an independent entity and make the decisions about size, resource deployment, and revenue levels itself based on its own perception about missions and markets. A certain amount of tension can be expected over the terms of the agreement between the center and the subunit. The center may, at times, seek to impose its own decisions on the subunits because the independence of the subunit is at the sufferance of the center. While the center has deliberately decided to allow local independence, it would take a central administration of rare consistency never to deviate from this policy. The center is also under pressure from its nonindependent subunits to be evenhanded in its policies, even if such evenhandedness is precluded by the agreement with the independent subunit. For example, a budget crisis that forces a salary freeze except in the independent subunit will lead to claims of inequity. There may also be constant friction over the range, cost, and central authority of services provided by the center. The subunit, for its part, tends to want it both ways—being able to tap the full resources of the center while retaining total control over the resources received.

Applications of Budgetary Incentives

This section demonstrates how the various models of budgetary incentives work in practice. Using actual budgetary systems and examining the incentives brought into play provides an insight that models of pure systems never can. Cases presented illustrate the latter three models; cases of the central-control model and the allocational formula model have been extensively documented over the years and further discussion here would add little.

The case analysis for each model describes one example with supplemental material added where needed. In each case, the discussion includes (1) a brief description of the organizational context of the budgetary system; (2) a discussion of the workings of the budgetary system itself; (3) an analysis of how the budgetary system does and does not fit the model it is being used to illustrate; (4) an analysis of the incentives induced by the budgetary system; and (5) some conclusions about the overall success of the budgetary system.

The Outcomes-Oriented Model in Practice. Outcomes-based funding has received a great deal of discussion over the past several years, but there have been few attempts to implement such a system on a comprehensive basis. State funding of private higher education has often been based on outcomes (specifically on the award of degrees). New York's Bundy Aid Program is a good example of such an approach (State Education Department, 1981) that has been replicated in other states. Another attempt to use outcomes-based incentives in a reasonably comprehensive budget system is the Tennessee Performance Budget project (Bogue, 1982). In many senses, this is one of the most determined efforts to use outcomes measures in budgeting that has ever been attempted. It has, however, been extensively discussed in the literature and will not be discussed here. I consider it to be the most interesting case of outcomes-based funding and urge readers to learn more about it.

The case study selected to illustrate the outcomes-based model of providing budgetary incentives is the Regents' Endowed Teachers and Scholars Program of the University of Texas ("UT's Endowed Faculty Posts . . . ," 1983). Supplementary illustrations are drawn from a similar program operated by the state of Virginia. The University of Texas is in the fortunate position of being massively endowed. The endowment is in the form of a "permanent university fund" established by the state of Texas in the 1880s. The principal of this fund is based on state lands whose revenue is pledged to the University of Texas (two-thirds) and Texas A&M (one-third). Like all endowments, the principal of the permanent university fund is not expendable, but the income is. Since the lands pledged to the fund were later found to have oil deposits, the annual income is large ($109 million for the University of Texas in 1983–84). The annual income is transferred to the "available university fund," which is expendable at the discretion of the regents of the University of Texas. The first call on these funds is to pay off the bonded indebtedness of the university. The annual requirements for this purpose were only $38 million in 1983–84, with the remainder of the funds being expendable for other purposes (Lasher, 1983). It is important to understand that the state does not take such funds into consideration in budgeting, and it makes no revenue deduction for funds realized from the available university fund. This fund is truly a supplemental (and large) source of funds for the regents. Even without this supplemental income, Texas treats public higher education rather generously—allocating 113 percent of the national per capita average to higher education; of course, this is offset by an equally high enrollment rate (McCoy and Halstead,

1982). The state of Virginia established a similar program from discretionary resources.

Using resources from the available university fund, the regents of the University of Texas match contributions made by private individuals, groups, or corporations who establish endowed faculty positions at the University of Texas at Austin. Such endowed chairs are established with a minimum contribution of $500,000, which provides sufficient annual income to pay a substantial portion of the expenses of the chair. For a $100,000 contribution, an endowed professorship may be established. The annual income from this fund is used to supplement the state-funded salary of a professor and may provide for additional perquisites, such as research support and professional travel. An endowed fellowship, a teaching fellowship, or visiting professorship can be established for $50,000 and a lectureship for $20,000. The donor may choose whether the matching funds (drawn by the regents from the available university fund) are to be used to support the endowed position or whether additional endowed positions are to be established ("UT's Endowed Faculty Posts . . . ," 1983).

While the donor may specify the use of the matching positions, the regents encourage that gifts be given to schools and colleges so that the regents may establish endowed positions where most needed. The regents also encourage the establishment of endowed fellowships and teaching fellowships to support promising but nonestablished faculty members. Finally, the regents retain a limited right to shift the funds of the endowed position. For example, when an endowed position is vacant, the regents will temporarily use the income for an endowed fellowship (Board of Regents, 1983). Matching funds transferred from the available university fund have been of the magnitude of $10 to $20 million annually (Lasher, 1983). Virginia's program is similar to that of Texas except that the matching funds are appropriated from state general revenues (State Council of Higher Education, undated).

The Regents' Endowed Teachers and Scholars Program at the University of Texas is a relatively simple attempt to provide incentives for producing specified outcomes. This simplicity represents one of the most important deviations from the outcomes-oriented model. The program does not represent a comprehensive approach to budgeting but is only an add-on incentive. This incentive, while large in absolute terms, is only a small fraction of the total institutional revenues available to the institution's schools and departments. It is, however, aimed at a critical area of academic decision making—the hiring and compensating of faculty members.

Another important area where the University of Texas program differs from the classical outcomes model has to do with the emphasis on producing outputs based on the quality of the inputs. Theoretically, the outcomes-oriented model is concerned neither with the inputs (the faculty in endowed positions) nor with controlling the target of expenditures. Nevertheless, when viewed from the traditional Texas higher education perspective that outcomes depend heavily on input quality, the Regents' Endowed Teachers and Scholars Program does qualify as a true outcomes-oriented model. The program represents a deviation from traditional practice in Texas; resources typically are aimed at obtaining solid faculty across the board. The scale of the program is sufficiently large that the two goals are beginning to merge. It should also be remembered that the faculty are not just another input in the educational process but are the heart of the institution. Since higher education has been described as an "organized anarchy" (Cohen and March, 1974) where each individual pursues his or her own interests, faculty conduct of instruction, research, and public service, in many ways, does represent an outcome of institutional practice. The restriction of the funds to the particular purpose is an artifact of the financial instrument used (endowments) and does not constitute a significant constraint.

The final significant deviation of the Regents' Endowed Teachers and Scholars Program from the classic outcomes-oriented model is some lack of clarity in the outcomes being sought. In part, this lack of clarity is eliminated by an understanding of the logic already described regarding the role of the faculty. In another way, though, the lack of clarity is real. The relationship between inputs and outcomes is imperfect even when the Texas philosophy is accepted. There is also lack of clarity between the pursuit of research outcomes and instructional outcomes. Much of the rhetoric of the program (used for fund raising) has to do with instruction; yet the nature of academia is that the distinguished faculty members have made their reputations through research. This distinction is, of course, blunted by the symbiotic relationship between instruction and research and by the efforts of the institution to use some of the resources for lectureships, teaching fellowships, and visiting professorships.

At one level, the incentives induced by the Regents' Endowed Scholars and Teachers Program are very simple. The schools and departments are strongly encouraged to concentrate their fund-raising efforts on improving the quality of the faculty. The hierarchy of endowed positions allows such efforts to be spread over a larger segment of potential donors to the university than would be the case if the only possibility were an endowed chair at $500,000. The importance of fund raising for eminent faculty is thus raised above fund raising for facilities, equipment, and student aid—the more traditional areas of fund-raising efforts.

At another level, however, the incentives induced by this program are more complex. First, as already noted, there may be a shift toward research outcomes and away from instructional outcomes based on the nature of the faculty recruited under the program, even though this is not the intent. Given the role and mission of the University of Texas at Austin, this may, of course, be entirely appropriate. Second, the faculty resource is declared the preeminent resource. This tends to increase the prestige and independence of the faculty. Third, the program, with its attendant publicity, has probably diverted resources from facilities construction. Maintenance requirements are also reduced in this way. Finally, the University of Texas has deliberately directed some of the resources generated by the program to promising junior faculty. This tends to avoid the most profound criticism of outcomes-oriented budgeting (the rich get richer), to avoid a bidding war with other institutions for a few faculty "stars," and to improve the overall outcomes of higher education (not just at the University of Texas) by developing younger faculty members.

As is the case with all outcomes-oriented approaches to budgeting, determining the success of the Regents' Endowed Teachers and Scholars Program is a difficult and lengthy process. It will be many years before all the outcomes produced by the program will have occurred, even if they could be measured easily. Indicators of the success of the program could be the change in the rankings of the University of Texas at Austin in the traditional peer evaluations of departmental quality, the flow of important research from the university, and the demand for Ph.D.s from the University of Texas for faculty appointments at other universities. All of these effects will take many years to become evident. By one measure, the Regents' Endowed Scholars and Teachers Program has already been spectacularly successful. In four years, the number of endowed positions has increased by 450 percent. Twenty-eight percent of all faculty at the university occupy endowed positions ("UT's Endowed Faculty Posts . . . ," 1983). If another institution in the country has matched this performance, the author is unaware of it.

The Good-Management-Practices Model in Practice. The case chosen to illustrate the good-management-practices approach to incentive financing is that of Northeast Missouri State University (NMSU). NMSU is a regional university offering a wide range of undergraduate programs and limited graduate study. The institution has received national attention, as well as additional resources from the state of Missouri, for its efforts in the area of value-added assessment of student learning. For the past ten years, a great deal of attention has been devoted to building a student data base that would allow such assessment and to analyzing the findings (Northeast Missouri State University, 1981). The approach to academic programming at NMSU over these years has been very much a classical outcomes-oriented approach. For the most part, however, the budget of the institution was not used as an incentive to accomplish the goals of the program. A combination of presidential leadership and central funding for the establishment of the necessary data base was used to establish the approach.

In the late 1970s, the Missouri Department of Higher Education and the governor's Office of Budgeting and Planning became interested in the idea of outcomes-oriented budgeting and asked institutions of higher education to request funds for the specific purpose of improving program quality. Because of the outcomes-oriented approach on campus and the existence of a substantial data base related to student achievement, NMSU was in an ideal position to respond to this request. The institution put together a supplemental budget request and received an additional $400,000 (about half of the request) as a result (Northeast Missouri State University, 1981). In subsequent years, NMSU has continued to pursue the practice of presenting their state budget request in an outcomes-oriented format (Northeast Missouri State University, 1982). In encouraging the institutions to submit such requests and in granting some of the requests, the state was adopting an outcomes-oriented approach to financial incentives. The focus in this section, however, is not on the state processes but on the further internal budgetary efforts at NMSU to extend the outcomes-oriented approach.

In discussing the budgetary incentives for good management practices at NMSU, we should note that the incentive finance system is only a very small part of the total budget and a very small part of the effort to use value-added concepts at the institution. Of the funds received from the state as a result of the special quality-improvement request, a small portion ($84,000) was not built into the regular expenditure base. Rather, these funds were kept centrally and used to operate a small grants program to assist academic units in their efforts to increase value added. The grants are intended to increase the effectiveness of existing academic resources and not to expand the resources available. For examples, grants have been given for consultants to assist departments in reorganizing their curriculum and in measuring the effect of the curriculum on students. In other cases, grants have been made for professional travel to assist faculty in their efforts to assess and improve value added. Funds have also been expended to help in the development of additional measures of achievement and to analyze testing results (Kruegar, 1983).

The budgetary system used by NMSU differs very little from the good-management-practices model. Funds are provided in return for performing certain activities that strengthen the ability of academic units to add value to the education provided. The NMSU budgetary system is unusual in that it is embedded in a comprehensive nonbudgetary effort to accomplish a larger goal.

The incentives generated by the grants program at NMSU encourage schools and departments to think creatively about furthering the goals of the value-added approach to instruction. Grants are used to fund innovations or refinements to the basic system of testing students and calculating value added. Individual faculty members and academic units are rewarded for suggesting such innovations and refinements by being given the additional resources.

The budgetary incentive portion of the value-added approach at NMSU is relatively new, and it is perhaps too soon to evaluate its success. It is clear, however, that the value-added approach continues to be expanded. A new value-added proposal to the state has been developed and has been submitted as a request (Kruegar, 1983).

The Full-Responsibility Model in Practice. The case study chosen to illustrate this model is the funding system used by the state of Colorado. Known from the instrument that implemented it as the Memorandum of Understanding (MOU) system, this financing scheme is designed to free institutions from detailed state budgetary controls.

The public higher education system in Colorado consists of seven governing boards controlling twenty-two institutions (plus four partially state-supported but locally controlled community colleges) and a multi-institution campus as well as a standard state coordinating agency (Colorado Commission on Higher Education, 1983). The budget process in Colorado is largely controlled by the legislature with the Joint Budget Committee playing the key role, the majority party (Republican) caucuses playing a secondary role, and everyone else having little impact. The MOU was developed to replace a system of detailed state budgetary control that had been in place for many years. The MOU was negotiated between the Joint Budget Committee and the higher education community with the coordinating agency playing a key brokering role (Hyde, 1983). The executive branch, although it lacks great power in the budgetary field, has substantial power over personnel (not including the faculty and top administration in higher education), purchasing, accounting, and the like (*Colorado Revised Statutes,* 1973).

The MOU budget system is based on the legislature making two fundamental decisions each year—how many in-state students are to be supported and what amount of state subsidy is to be provided. To date, the legislature has decided to provide support for all in-state students enrolling at Colorado public institutions; only enrollments at the two research universities are limited (Hyde, 1983). The amount of support provided per student has been an extrapolation of average support levels existing before the MOU. The amount varies by governing board and in some cases by institution based on the historic role and mission of the institutions (Joint Budget Committee, 1983). Other budgetary decisions, with several exceptions, are left to the governing boards. The boards set tuition rates, have complete freedom on admission of out-of-state students, retain all income from tuition and other sources, roll funds forward from year to year, make allocations among campuses, schools, and departments, among functions, and among objects of expenditure, and set salary patterns for non-civil service employees. The exceptions to the governing boards' authority are as follows: (1) control over civil service employees' salaries are vested in the state Department of Personnel; (2) power over accounting/reporting conventions, data processing purchases/leases, and other purchasing are vested with the state Department of Administration; (3) limitations are set on the numbers of faculty and "administrators" that can be hired; (4) out-of-state tuition must be at least three times in-state tuition; and (5) capital construction is still done on a project-by-project basis by the legislature (Joint Budget Committee, 1983).

The actual funding system used is the appropriation by the legislature of a certain number of dollars per in-state FTE student times the number of such students estimated by the Colorado Commission on Higher Education. Appropriations for the coming year are made in the spring, corrected for enrollment changes in the spring of the current year, and corrected again for final enrollments in the spring of the following year. The funding per in-state FTE student is determined by applying a standard percentage increase to the per-student amount received by the boards in the prior year and has been changed in midyear only when revenue shortfalls force a state budget reduction. In this case, the per-student figure is reduced by a standard percentage. The funding base upon which the per-student funding is based is derived from the earlier formula that considered role and mission, program and student mix, and administrative needs. The old formula used these factors to derive a total institutional expenditure base from which institutional revenues (for example, tuition or indirect cost recovery) were deducted. Because the MOU funding system considers only the state general fund, tuition differentials arising since the MOU was adopted are not reflected in appropriations, but pre-MOU tuition differentials are considered (Allen, 1983).

The Colorado MOU budgeting system does not completely fit the definition of the full-responsibility model. First, as already noted, the executive branch maintains significant control over the institutions. The controls do not greatly intrude on the primary functions of the institution, but they do have a substantial effect on the overall management of the institution. This is particularly true of the power exercised by the personnel department, whose rules and pay scales control approximately half of an institution's employees. Since the actions of the governing boards are centrally constrained, full responsibility does not exist. The incentives of the boards are clearly affected by the rules of the executive branch agencies.

Second, the MOU is reviewed annually and changes are made each year. Some of the changes are technical while others are seen as perfecting the MOU system. To date, fundamental changes have not been made but are clearly possible. It is also possible that the legislative branch would fail to honor its commitments or that executive-branch action would abrogate some provision of the MOU. During 1982-83, both the executive and legislative branches discussed recapturing cash reserves held by the governing board under the provisions of the Memorandum of Understanding (Perrin, 1983). Such discussions create a major barrier to the proper operations of the incentives that are supposed to be induced by the full-responsibility model.

Finally, and most importantly, old habits of thought fade slowly. Most individuals in state government, in both the executive and legislative branches, still regard the institutions as an integral part of state government. Although budgetary allocations are made on the basis of the MOU, many other decisions are made and issues are framed as if the institutions were still subject to line-item control (Hyde, 1983). Tuition levels are a source of constant legislative concern although they are theoretically outside the sphere of legislative control. Statutes continue to be passed placing authority over some function in a central agency regardless of higher education's "independence."

Interestingly enough, though, these tendencies are not the major constraints on institutions' actions. The major constraint lies in the habits of thought of the governing boards and their staff. Only two of the governing board systems can be said to have adopted fully the idea that they are completely responsible for their own systems. The other boards can be seen doing such things as carrying almost no reserves forward into a new fiscal year, advocating steps that could lead to the establishment of a state personnel system for faculty, and using the old state allocational formula for budget control purposes. The other boards have adopted many habits of thought of the new system but have not yet completely converted. The lack of such new habits of thought places constraints on the boards' imagination and ability to respond to the incentives provided.

In order to analyze the incentives brought into play by the MOU funding system, one must examine both revenues and expenditures. The most important variable on the revenue side is enrollment of in-state students. State appropriation increments to institutions are based entirely on the number of FTE students enrolled. The amount per student varies according to role and mission and the mix of students and programs as of 1980-81 (Allen, 1983). Prior to the budget year, the Long Appropriations Bill is passed with a certain enrollment assumption embedded. The appropriation is updated in the spring of the budget year and again after the budget year is over with adjustments being made. The clear incentive provided by the state is for institutions to increase their enrollments, and institutions have attempted to respond. They have advertised in the media, recruited in the high schools, attempted to retain existing students, structured tuition rates so as to encourage enrollment for more credit hours, begun new and attractive programs, and, in the case of the University of Colorado-Boulder and of Colorado State University, sought release from limits on their enrollments. It is difficult to judge the success of those institutional efforts in light of larger demographic, social, and economic change, but institutions clearly have attempted to increase enrollments, and one should assume that some successes have occurred, if only in shifting enrollments among institutions.

In retrospect, it is not altogether clear whether the state meant to provide such a strong incentive regarding enrollments. The state enrollment policy is demand-driven (except for the University of Colorado-Boulder and Colorado State University, which are capped). Various attempts to move away from a demand-driven enrollment model have been made, as exemplified by the Colorado Commission on Higher Education policy study proposed in its master plan (Colorado Commission on Higher Education, 1983). For now, however, enrollment increases are rewarded and decreases punished.

The incentive for enrollment increases has been substantially strengthened by the use of an average-cost mechanism for funding such increases. It is reasonable to assume that, in the range of enrollment change being discussed, marginal cost is less than average cost. For growing institutions, this differential generates a surplus that can be used for new programs, increased faculty salaries, library materials, and the like. For a shrinking institution, the opposite is true (Allen and Brinkman, 1983). Discussion has occurred about adoption of a marginal-costing mechanism, but such discussion has been limited.

Another set of incentives regarding enrollments surrounds the two institutions that have enrollment caps. The University of Colorado-Boulder and Colorado State University are limited to a specified number of in-state FTE students. They may exceed this limit by 1.5 percent of their enrollment without any change in their appropriation. If they grow by more than that amount, they receive an appropriation penalty for each additional student (Joint Budget Committee, 1983). While this provides a strong incentive not to exceed the cap, the difficulties of managing a large institution to a specific FTE level and the desire to accommodate as many students as possible have led one institution to one imposed penalty and numerous close calls. It may be that the marginal cost of educating the additional student who is within the allowed variance is less than the tuition revenue received, and this tempts the institutions to be as close to the limit as possible. It may also be part of the institutions' efforts to serve as many Colorado students as they can.

There is an explicit agreement on the part of the institutions not to seek funding beyond the per-student amount either as part of the regular appropriations or of the supplemental process. This arrangement strengthens the enrollment incentive but also reaffirms that the institutions are responsible for the management of their own fiscal affairs; a state "bailout" cannot be expected. A limited possibility of state financial rescue is provided for only in the event of another utility price explosion. Institutions are thus encouraged to carry forward cash reserves from year to year. Further, although nonrenewal of the MOU would stop further increases in the cash reserves, it would not permit recapture of existing cash reserves. Nevertheless, the recent discussion about recapturing reserves has left the institutions wondering about the wisdom of holding large amounts. Institutions could, of course, transfer the reserves to noncurrent funds and out of the direct sight of state budget makers.

The other major source of unrestricted institutional revenue is that of tuition and fees. The MOU provides that the governing boards have almost complete discretion over this source of revenue. They may set tuition and fees at any level, use any structure, make changes at any time (for example, midyear) and use all revenue generated at their own discretion. The only restriction is that out-of-state tuition must be at least three times in-state tuition, and even this rule can be waived by the Colorado Commission on Higher Education, which has never refused a request to do so. The clear incentive is to generate as much tuition revenue as possible. The institution thus tends to set tuition rates at what the market will bear. For in-state students, tuition price is largely determined by prices charged by other Colorado public institutions and by the values of board members. Thus, except at one unique institution, tuition increases have been moderate.

In the case of tuition revenue from out-of-state students, market considerations are rather more complex. Each institution competes in the national marketplace. Tuition prices are not limited by in-state competition or by the public pressures. Estimates of the price elasticity of revenue are made and used in tuition setting (Fischer, 1983).

All other revenues to the institutions are beyond state control except for a statutory provision that interest income on funds deposited in the state treasury accrue to the state general fund. This provision weakens the financial incentives for the institutions to build cash balances but has not visibly reduced institutional efforts to maintain such balances. It is worth noting, however, that the largest balances are held by the one governing board that is exempt from depositing its funds in the state treasury (Hyde, 1983).

On the expenditure side of the equation, what is striking in the MOU system is not the provision of incentives to do particular things but the lack of disincentives to take full responsibility. The institutions have responded to the lack of disincentives by shifting funds among categories to meet internal priorities. With two major exceptions, however, the institutional response on the expenditure side has not matched that on the revenue side, perhaps because the incentives to do so are not as strong.

One institution, pressed by a major enrollment/revenue crisis, has engaged in a major academic renewal process (University of Northern Colorado, 1982). Two other governing boards have systematically attempted to build areas of excellence and rectify longstanding problems with faculty salaries, library acquisitions, and instructional equipment. The other boards have made minor adjustments but have basically pursued a business-as-usual approach on the expenditure side (Hyde, 1983).

Although only limited constraints are put on institutional expenditure patterns, significant administrative controls remain and provide disincentives or outright prohibitions on efficient use of resources. The most important one of these is the setting of salaries statewide for about half the institutions' employees. All ways to reduce the impact of such wages on institutions' budgets are legally constrained except elimination of positions. Thus, a significant incentive for support staff attrition is provided.

The overall success of the Colorado model has to be rated as conditional. Two of the governing boards have responded fully to the incentives provided and are functioning as independently and responsibly as the overall system allows. The other four boards have not responded in a comprehensive manner. In part, this is attributable to the habits of thought of board members and staff. The two boards with the strongest use of the MOU govern those institutions that could best function entirely without state support. It may be, however, that the other four boards have more accurately perceived the fragility of the MOU and have correctly anticipated that only with limited responses will the MOU system be preserved in the long run.

Conclusion

Budgetary incentives to accomplish central goals can be powerful tools that are far less disruptive of administrative processes and program goals than is detailed central control. The case studies have shown various achievements, and there are many other possibilities in theory and in current use. Nevertheless, the use of budgetary incentives to accomplish central goals has several serious limitations.

The budget is an imperfect instrument. A budget system that is comprehensive in its attempt to use incentives to accomplish a large number of the center's goals will, of necessity, be so complex that many dysfunctional or irrelevant incentives may be created accidentally. No comprehensive budgetary system can ever anticipate all the incentives created. No new incentive budgetary system can ever overcome the iron law of budgeting, which is that budgets are fundamentally incremental. No budgetary system can ever be so comprehensive as to eliminate extra-budgetary incentives (salary setting, receipt of external grants, professional standards, legal considerations, and so on). The effort required to build a fully comprehensive system is so large that it is seldom attempted and probably never accomplished.

One alternative to a comprehensive budgetary system is a small grants program designed to affect only a small but, one hopes, critical component of subunit behavior. If the behavioral component is chosen carefully, the grants program can have influence out of proportion to its size, but it also must be recognized that a grants program, unless it is very large, can never have a comprehensive impact. The University of Texas program described in this chapter comes as close to having a comprehensive impact as probably any grants program is ever likely to achieve.

Another interesting alternative is the radical decentralization proposed in the full-responsibility model. In its purest form, this model almost denies the concept of a central organization. It relies instead on a market-type model with the center serving only to police the market and define the unit of exchange. In the case of the Colorado system described here, the unit of exchange was in-state FTE students. It would be the rare central administration that would define itself out of existence as a matter of principle.

A state or institution seeking to implement incentive financing should begin on a modest scale. A good place to start would be to eliminate some of the worst *disincentives* to responsible behavior—for example, central capture of incremental revenues earned by a subunit and requirements for lapses of unexpended funds at the end of a fiscal period. A small grants program aimed at important behavioral factors would be the next logical step. Following this, grants programs could be expanded in numbers and size with continued reviews being conducted. A comprehensive system should be attempted only with great caution.

References

Allen, R. "Linkage Between APCUP Formulas and Actual Funding." Unpublished manuscript, Denver, Colo., 1983.
Allen, R., and Brinkman, P. *Marginal Costing Techniques for Higher Education.* Boulder, Colo.: National Center for Higher Education Management Systems, 1983.
Baldridge, J. V., Curtis, D. V., Ecker, G., and Riley, G. L. *Policy Making and Effective Leadership: A National Study of Academic Management.* San Francisco: Jossey-Bass, 1978.
Board of Regents. Minutes of meeting. Austin, Tex., October 13-14, 1983.
Bogue, E. G. "Allocation of Public Funds on Instructional Performance/Quality Indicators." *The International Journal of Institutional Management in Higher Education,* 1982, *6,* 37-43.
Cohen, M. D., and March, J. G. *Leadership and Ambiguity: The American College President.* New York: McGraw-Hill, 1974.

Colorado Commission on Higher Education. *Colorado-Statewide Master Plan for Postsecondary Education: 1983-1984 Through 1986-1987.* Denver, Colo.: Colorado Commission on Higher Education, 1983.

Curry, D., Fischer, N., and Jons, T. "State Policy Options for Financing Higher Education and Related Accountability Objectives." Paper presented to the Washington Council on Postsecondary Education, Olympia, 1982.

Fayol, H. *General and Industrial Management.* (C. Storrs, trans.) London: Pitman, 1949.

Fischer, W. Personal communication. Denver, Colo., July 12, 1983.

Hambrick, D. C., and Mason, P. A. "Organization as a Reflection of Its Top Managers." *Annual Proceedings of the Academy of Management,* 1982, 12-16.

Hyde, W. "Providing Public Colleges and Universities More Fiscal Autonomy: The Experience in Colorado." Denver, Colo.: Education Commission of the States, 1983.

Joint Budget Committee. *1983-84 Appropriations Report.* Denver: State of Colorado Joint Budget Committee, 1983.

Kruegar, D. Personal communication, October 19, 1983.

Lasher, W. Personal communication, November 12, 1983.

McCoy, M. and Halstead, D. K. *Higher Education Financing in the Fifty States: Interstate Comparisons Fiscal Year 1979.* Boulder, Colo.: National Center for Higher Education Management Systems, 1982.

McKeon, R. M. "Suboptimization Criteria and Operations Research." In M. Alexis and C. Z. Wilson (Eds.), *Organizational Decision Making.* Englewood Cliffs, N. J.: Prentice-Hall, 1967.

Mintzberg, H. *The Structuring of Organizations: A Synthesis of the Research.* Englewood Cliffs, N.J.: Prentice-Hall, 1979.

Northeast Missouri State University. *Program Improvements as a Part of Northeast Missouri State University's Funding.* Kirksville: Northeast Missouri State University, 1981.

Northeast Missouri State University. *Appropriation Request: Fiscal Year 1984.* Kirksville: Northeast Missouri State University, 1982.

Perrin, J. Personal communication, June 3, 1983.

Roethlisberger, F. J., and Dickson, W. J. *Management and the Worker.* Cambridge, Mass.: Harvard University Press, 1939.

State Council of Higher Education. *Policies and Procedures for Allocating State Matching Funds under Item 201, 1982 Appropriation Act—Eminent Scholars Program.* Richmond, Va.: State Council of Higher Education, undated.

State Education Department. *New York State Bundy Aid Program: 1969-1981.* Albany, N.Y.: State Education Department, 1981.

State of Colorado. *Colorado Revised Statutes.* Denver: State of Colorado, 1973.

University of Northern Colorado. *A Plan for the Future.* Greeley: University of Northern Colorado, 1982.

"UT's Endowed Faculty Posts Lead Nation." *Campus Cameo,* 1983, pp. 56-57.

Weber, M. *Theory of Social and Economic Organization.* Glencoe, N.Y.: 1947.

Richard H. Allen is associate budget director, University of Colorado.

An analysis of resource reduction and reallocation strategies forms the basis for ten observations about the content and impact of budget cuts and the effectiveness of different strategies.

Budgeting Strategies Under Conditions of Decline

Kenneth P. Mortimer
Barbara E. Taylor

This chapter analyzes resource reduction and reallocation strategies and tactics in four-year colleges and universities. That there is a need for more effective ways to deal with resource scarcity, environmental uncertainty, and institutional rigidities has been well established in other chapters in this volume and elsewhere (Mortimer and Tierney, 1979), and it will not be repeated here.

Several different sources make up the basis for the observations offered here. An extensive review of the literature on reduction and reallocation experiences has been in process since 1979. In addition, a number of research studies and projections on faculty reductions and retrenchment have been published in professional journals, books, and monographs (Johnson and Mortimer, 1977; Mortimer and Tierney, 1979; and Mortimer, 1981).

In the summer of 1982, with the support of the Lilly Endowment, a national sample of 318 chief academic officers in four-year colleges and universities was interviewed by telephone. The interviews ranged from twenty minutes to two hours, with the most common being thirty or forty minutes in length. (The original sample included 369 institutions. The 318 interviews represent a response rate of 86 percent.)

The interview responses were matched with other institutional information, such as enrollment history, Carnegie classification, public/private status, and so forth. The result is a data file on institutional experience with faculty staffing and reduction policies, program closures and additions, and the processes of academic budgeting. This chapter draws on the information gathered on budgeting strategies.

Finally, during the 1982 and 1983 academic years, site visits of from three days to one week were conducted at nine institutions. The purpose of these visits was to probe the dynamics of institutional adaptation to conditions of uncertainty and decline. The nine site visits included four independent and five public institutions, and all were chosen for their heuristic value. No attempt was made to be representative in the pure sense, but the institutions were spread from New England to California. Three of the institutions had engaged in layoffs of tenured faculty, one reorganized four schools into two major faculties, and another was using program reviews in its reallocation process. One institution served as an example of academic renewal through serving new clientele, and still another served as an example of an attempt to upgrade the image of academic quality by seeking accreditation for its business programs.

The first section in this chapter analyzes the contexts of the institutional condition that may apply in given situations. The terms reduction, reallocation, and retrenchment are used to describe these contexts, but it should be noted that one or all of the three may be characteristic of a given institution at a particular time.

The second section concentrates on reviewing the case literature on budgeting strategies under conditions of decline through the lens of two analytic continuums: across-the-board versus selective budget cutting and the use of attrition versus decremental budgeting devices.

The final section draws on the first two but concentrates on ten lessons learned from the site visits. These observations are offered as conventional wisdom on the context of budget cuts, the strengths and weaknesses of various reduction and reallocation devices, and consultation under general conditions of scarcity.

Institutional Context

Each institution must have an accurate assessment of its resources for the coming decade. For heuristic purposes, we identify three probable institutional needs that are determined by institutional context—the need to reallocate resources, people, and programs in response to changing student demand; the need to reduce institutional size and/or faculty over a reasonable period of time; and the need to retrench faculty in the very short run.

Reallocation. Perhaps the most complex ingredient in an institutional faculty profile is trying to develop responses to shifts in student demand. The magnitude of these shifts is indicated by the following enrollment data (Stadtman, 1980):

From 1969 to 1976 undergraduate major enrollments in the professions rose by 53 percent (from 38 percent to 58 percent of the total) whereas enrollment in humanities majors dropped 44 percent (from 9 percent to 5 percent) and in the social sciences by 33 percent (from 18 percent to 12 percent). When the number of faculty is considered by majors, however, one finds an increase of only 16 percent in the professions and a decline of only 5 percent in the humanities, while there has been no change in the percentage of faculty teaching in the social sciences.

One could conclude from these data that institutions have not been successful in reallocating faculty resources into the major fields where enrollment growth is occurring. It should be noted, however, that not all enrollments occur in major fields and that the humanities and social sciences are important complementary ingredients in many undergraduate professional degree programs.

On the other hand, the apparent imbalances in faculty resources should not be dismissed by blind support for the liberal or general education of candidates for professional degrees. The conflict between liberal arts and professional areas is well illustrated by the following quotation about the University of Colorado at Boulder (Jedamus, 1980):

> In 1967 to 1977, student credit hours in business doubled, while business faculty increased by less than 10 percent. If the institution had been growing overall, the strain would not have been as severe, but with enrollment capped, reallocation of [full-time equivalent students] FTEs from arts and science to business proved well near impossible. One consequence was that the college of business had to impose severe restrictions on its enrollment in order to maintain its accreditation. . . . The college had to refuse admission to some 2,000 qualified applicants for the fall of 1979. SCH/FTE faculty production in the college of business is about 50 percent higher than that of arts and science and among the highest of comparable colleges of business.
>
> In spite of these facts, when it was proposed by the administration that no cuts be made in the college of business faculty, the powerful lobbying block of arts and science insisted that the cuts be made proportionately among all colleges regardless of faculty loads (p. 43).

This incident is not isolated. The business school faculty at Temple University filed a grievance under their union contract asserting that their teaching loads were heavier on the average than those in liberal arts and that this difference was unfair and unreasonable. In another major public university, student credit hours per faculty member in the school of business are the highest in the university and are more than twice as high as those in two other professional schools.

Reduction in Size. Some institutions will find it necessary to reduce the size of their faculties in the coming years. For example, an analysis (Otzenberger and Kaelke, 1980) of Montana State University's (MSU) potential showed that:

> MSU will, over the next ten years, face reductions in the size of the faculty greater than the number of openings created by retirement. Because the national job market may also be very bleak, it was further assumed that faculty members will attempt to remain in their present jobs for as long as possible. The extreme version of this assumption, that no resignations will be submitted except for retirement, projects a very bleak picture in which perhaps an average of twelve faculty members per year will have to be involuntarily terminated. Further, if tenure is granted to 90 percent of those currently "on track," the entire faculty could conceivably be tenured (p. 5).

Johnstone (1980) reports that the staffing ratio at Montana State University had gone from fourteen to one in 1960 to nineteen to one in 1979 and implies that it has reached its limit. Minter and Bowen's (1982) national surveys report only a slight change in the ratio of faculty members to students; full-time equivalents were about 1 to 14.7 in 1969–70 and 1 to 14.1 in 1979–80. We found numerous cases where student-faculty ratios became the focus of fiscal control also. Hruby (1973) suggests in his monograph on Aquinas College that this was part of that college's struggle for financial stability.

There are only three basic ways to increase the student-faculty ratio: either increase the number of students and hold the number of faculty constant, reduce the number of faculty and hold the number of students constant, or develop some combination of the two. These various combinations have distinctly different income and expenditure implications. In an era of declining resources, specifically in enrollments, many institutions will find it necessary to reduce faculty just to maintain established student-faculty ratio policies.

Retrenchment. There is some confusion about the term retrenchment. As used here, it means the dismissal or layoff of tenured faculty, or of nontenured faculty in midcontract. We have discussed faculty retrenchment elsewhere and summarize that discussion here (Mortimer and Tierney, 1979; Mortimer, 1981).

Three basic questions dominate the national discussion:
1. Under what conditions should (or could) faculty be dismissed or laid off?
2. What procedures are necessary or desirable in retrenchment?
3. What criteria should be used?

The argument over retrenchment conditions tends to revolve around what constitutes authentic financial emergency and program discontinuance, since virtually all parties agree that faculty may be terminated for cause or medical reasons. The American Association of University Professors (AAUP) advocates a definition of financial exigency that involves a threat to institutional survival whereas others would adopt a less stringent definition (see Gray, 1981, for a discussion of court cases on this matter).

Our discussions with chief academic officers in public institutions and the survey of recent literature lead us to the conclusion that financial emergency is a more useful term than exigency. Emergency conveys the relative lack of time to deal with the rapidly changing circumstances involved with revenue shortfalls while an exigent situation may refer to general conditions of decline.

The emergency condition of revenue shortfalls is becoming increasingly common in the public sector of American higher education. Mingle (1982) reports that, "Three times in the past ten years, economic downturns have been severe enough to cause abrupt midyear curtailments of spending plans in some states, as tax collections dropped with the declining economy. The first substantial cutbacks affecting higher education occurred in the 1974-75 recession, the second in 1979-80, and states face similar circumstances in 1982. (Ten southern states have been affected in the last two years)" (p. 1).

The problem in the private sector is how to deal with general decline. The most common cases are when "paid accepts" fall drastically in one year. One chief academic officer lamented in the summer of 1982 that fall enrollment was going to be fifty students less than planned. A $250,000 shortfall in a small college budget will require drastic adjustments during the year.

Bowen and Glenny (1976) have made eight recommendations on the steps institutions can use during such emergency conditions. Briefly, institutions have to consider the advantages of selective as opposed to across-the-board reductions, the limits on flexibility represented by fixed costs, the appropriate student and faculty consultative mechanisms, rules and regulations that limit fiscal flexibility, and procedures for faculty layoff and reallocation. Other guidelines to be followed in times of retrenchment can be found in Fortunato and Waddell (1981) and Melchiori (1982).

The terms reallocation, reduction, and retrenchment refer, then, to institutional context and specific conditions. In the following section, we discuss the strategies and managerial devices used to cope with these contexts.

Budget Strategies and Their Effectiveness

Institutions experiencing financial shortfalls respond in varying ways to their predicament. Fundamentally, budget strategies under conditions of decline assume either an across-the-board or a selective focus, and they employ attrition or decremental budget cuts to compensate for the shortfall. In fact, institutions in financial difficulty often employ some combination of these strategies, whether simultaneously or sequentially.

Across-the-Board Strategies. Furman (1981) points out that across-the-board strategies involving all segments of all institutional budgets are encountered rarely. More commonly, portions of both nonacademic and academic budgets are assigned specific across-the-board reductions. All faculty personnel budgets, for example, are treated identically, regardless of department. All clerical personnel budgets are also treated identically, but perhaps differently from the faculty budgets.

Across-the-board reductions offer an appealing solution to budget shortfalls. They are easy to apply, appear humanitarian and democratic, and cause relatively less acrimony than selective cuts (Balderston, 1974; Glenny, 1982). The across-the-board approach may also be an appropriate response to modest, temporary budget shortfalls (Balderston, 1974). Some institutional leaders fear, moreover, that planning for selective budget or program cuts will create a "self-fulfilling prophecy" in which activities that might otherwise have survived fail because constituents, fearing the activities will fail, withdraw their support (Bowen and Glenny, 1981).

Detractors maintain, however, that across-the-board cuts are ultimately destructive to the institution. Dougherty (1981) argues first that the across-the-board approach assumes the budget is distributed equitably and that equal cuts will produce equal effects among all units. In fact, institutional priorities change, and allocations should change accordingly. Second, in treating strong and weak programs equally, the approach undermines the institution's strongest faculty. Finally, the approach discourages initiative because it provides no reallocated funds for new programs and even threatens such new efforts with future budget cuts.

Balderston (1974) and Glenny (1982) argue that reliance on across-the-board cuts often results in a crucial loss of time. When successive across-the-board reductions have weakened the institution's most vital programs and selective priorities for funding must be established, planning is necessarily done in an atmosphere of crisis. Moreover, selective priorities are more difficult to effect under such conditions because crucial slack resources that allow institutions to build programs have been sacrificed in earlier across-the-board reductions (Bowen and Glenny, 1981).

Across-the-Board Attrition. Expenditures are reduced through attrition when the institution decides not to replace personnel who resign or retire, defers building maintenance, or fails to replenish depleted stores of supplies. Across-the-board attrition, in which, for example, hiring and spending freezes are applied indiscriminately to all academic units, is seen frequently in colleges and universities, particularly in the first years of financial shortfall (Bowen and Glenny, 1981; Dickmeyer, 1983).

It is easy to understand why across-the-board attrition is so popular. Lee (1981) points out that institutions make the least disruptive budget cuts first and "only reluctantly proceed to cuts which are . . . not easily replaced" (p. 9). Institutional decision makers reason that they can always buy chalk next year but cannot so readily rebuild a closed foreign language program. In general, across-the-board strategies are seen as equitable; attrition is seen as humane. The combination is irresistible to most institutions.

Few institutions imagine that financial shortfalls will be long lived or pervasive (Bowen and Glenny, 1981; Lee, 1981), and attrition seems a reasonable short-term response. If shortfalls continue, however, the disadvantages of the approach become apparent. First, attrition is at best a random occurrence and at worst strikes where it does most damage (Dougherty, 1981; Glenny, 1982). Lack of supplies and inadequate maintenance may cause all to suffer equally, but the computer science department is far more likely to be damaged by the loss of a faculty member than is the philosophy department. The nature of the faculty labor market all but guarantees that attrition will occur most often in the wrong departments. Only over the long run is attrition likely to reduce or eliminate low-priority programs (Glenny, 1982). In the meantime, institutions relying on the strategy may see their morale and financial reserves depleted.

Across-the-Board Decrements. Nearly as common as across-the-board attrition, and often accompanying it, is the application of across-the-board decremental funding, in which all budgets or certain items in them are cut by some percentage. Glenny (1982) mentions travel, maintenance, and equipment purchases as particular "targets of opportunity" for decremental funding. Bowen and Glenny (1981) have found that clerical and administrative cutbacks and decremental funding of travel, maintenance, and other "operational" items were the most common responses to financial stress in the ten California colleges and universities they studied.

Across-the-board decrements are frequently a response to unexpected revenue shortfalls or recisions. Ohio State University, facing an unanticipated shortfall in state appropriations for the 1981–1982 academic year, planned across-the-board cuts in the nonteaching portion of all educational and general budgets. Ohio State's scheme was intended to protect the quality of the instructional program and to produce no "irreversible" results (Ihrig, 1983). Ohio State saw the shortfall as temporary, moved to protect its most central functions, and then to allocate the shortfall proportionately among all units. Equipment and other special purchases were to be deferred.

Similarly, the University of Kansas faced a 4 percent recision of state funding, announced in July 1982 and effective for the 1982–83 academic year. According to Hammond and Tompkins (1983), the university determined to cut the budget of academic units by 2.2 percent overall and nonacademic and administrative budgets by 4.3 percent. The central administration decided, furthermore, that no personnel would be dismissed and no salaries decreased. As a result, "equal" cuts had quite unequal results on individual departments. Departments with vacant positions or large equipment budgets made their cuts with less apparent difficulty than departments whose funds were committed almost entirely to personnel.

Pennsylvania State University applied annual across-the-board budget reductions to academic units between 1971 and 1976. Lozier and Althouse (1983) suggest that the approach simultaneously fostered erosion of high-quality, growing programs and assigned too great a share of scarce resources to declining activities. The Penn State experience illustrates the fundamental weakness of across-the-board decremental budget strategies. Repeatedly applied, such strategies maintain weak activities at the expense of strong ones. As emergency, one-time actions they may not damage the institution irreparably. Realizing this, Ohio State's planned "worst case" budget for the year following across-the-board cuts would have involved reallocations and would not have guaranteed protection of the entire institutional budget (Ihrig, 1983).

Selective Strategies. Bowen and Glenny (1981) conclude their study of response to financial stress in ten California colleges and universities by arguing that all institutions should develop procedures to determine relative personnel and program priorities. By establishing funding priorities, institutions can respond to budget shortfalls without irreparably weakening their most essential programs. While Balderston (1974) admits that establishing selective program priorities is difficult and often distressing, he argues that "the alternatives are worse" (p. 226). Across-the-board approaches weaken both strong and already marginal programs.

On the other hand, Balderston argues that selective strategies will not work without:

(1) the technical capability to analyze costs, interactions, and goal contributions of programs, and access to comparative

data to buttress the findings; (2) a way of joining credible and expert academic judgments with fiscal information; (3) an institutional process that meets conditions of fairness; and (4) a quality and range of academic and administrative leadership that can reach and enforce decisions without losing the ability to function in the future (p. 227).

Selective Attrition. Selective attrition allows slow budget reductions or reallocations of resources from marginal or lower-priority activities to areas of strength and high priority. Institutions that exercise central control over vacant positions, for example, may decide not to replace a retiring history professor, while they authorize the business administration department to hire additional faculty.

The success of selective attrition depends largely on luck and slack resources. If attrition occurs where it is most needed, the institution can make important adjustments painlessly. If, as is more likely, attrition occurs too slowly or in the wrong places, slack resources are needed to build and maintain crucial programs while continuing to support marginal or overbuilt activities. Few institutions boast significant slack resources.

Millington (1981) expresses the spirit of selective attrition when he writes of Stanford University's budgeting strategy: "We find increasing financial strength by reinforcing the winners and making support for marginal or poor performers more tentative" (pp. 93-94). Michigan State University pushed such "tentativeness" somewhat further in its 1981 "buy-outs" of approximately 100 tenured faculty members who might otherwise have been terminated during a financial crisis at the university. Incentives to resign, retire, or accept part-time tenure were offered to gain the cooperation of the faculty members in question, and they enabled Michigan State to orchestrate a substantial selective attrition (Kreinin, 1982).

Selective Decrements. When resource reallocations are perceived as the only reasonable way for the institution to meet actual or impending budget shortfalls, selective attrition by itself is seldom adequate to the task. Most colleges and universities would find the approach too slow and intolerably costly. Consequently, most institutions that have made selective cuts have done so through decremental program funding.

The literature reveals at least three approaches to selective decremental funding. These are: (1) the imposition of standard budget "targets" on each of the institution's units and the reallocation of these funds to high-priority programs; (2) the imposition of variable targets to create a reallocation fund; and (3) reallocations that follow priorities identified through a program review process.

The University of Michigan's Priority Fund (Mortimer and Tierney, 1979) is the best-known example of the *standard budget target* approach to reallocation. The base budget of each unit of the university is reduced by 1 percent each year. This provides a fund to support new or high-demand programs, equipment purchases, and other initiatives. While Michigan's system resembles an across-the-board decremental budgeting system, there are important differences. The yield from the 1 percent assessment is not used to finance deficits or to cover general university operating expenses, but rather to fund particular academic priorities. Moreover, Mortimer and Tierney explain that requests for priority funds are more often honored if the unit agrees to match the award with an internal reallocation of its own funds. Consequently, the priority fund's true effect on reallocation is magnified well beyond the 1 percent level.

Pennsylvania State University also relies on a target system for reallocation, but the targets are variable. Individual targets are assigned to institutional units according to such factors as enrollment shifts, program quality, need, centrality, management effectiveness, demand, productivity, and cost (Lozier and Althouse, 1983). Targets for any individual unit may vary from year to year, but they are estimated five years in advance. This enables the unit to plan to meet future assessments.

Between its inception in 1977 and five years later in 1982, Penn State's selective reallocation process had moved $16.6 million, primarily into high-priority academic areas. Mandated cost increases have been financed largely with other funds. Approximately one-third of the reallocated funds have come from academic areas and the remaining two-thirds from academic support and nonacademic areas.

Like the University of Michigan, Oklahoma State University chose to create a fund of reallocated monies to finance excellent and potentially excellent programs and initiatives. While the president, vice-presidents, and deans were assessed in 1977 an overall target amounting to 2 percent of their 1975 educational and general budget, individual units were assigned varying targets at the discretion of responsible administrators (Robl, Karman, and Boggs, 1976).

The programs and initiatives supported with Oklahoma's "excellence fund" are identified through a self-study process. Each unit ranks its programs according to their centrality, productivity, demand, cost, vitality, and uniqueness. The unit also indicates what it would do with more, fewer, or stable resources. Priority lists from each unit are combined and realigned at the college and university levels, and excellence funds are distributed accordingly.

Lozier and Althouse (1983) suggest that the target approach to reallocation may eventually lead to erosion in program quality. They conclude that "dramatic reassessment and change involving both substantial reductions and closures" may be necessary, particularly if significant state revenue shortfalls occur (p. 248). Such shortfalls were crucial factors in reallocation decisions at two campuses of the State University of New York and also at the University of Washington and the University of Minnesota. All four universities employed *program reviews* as the basis for making reallocation decisions.

The State University of New York (SUNY) campuses at Albany and Binghamton faced a common financial crisis in fiscal years 1976 and 1977 as the state's allocations to higher education were severely and suddenly curtailed in order to provide financial relief to a nearly bankrupt New York City (La Tourette, n.d.; Shirley, 1982). La Tourette adds, moreover, that SUNY's chancellor and vice-chancellor required the 1977 fiscal year reductions to be selective and also directed reallocation to areas of strength and high potential. Reductions and reallocations of 3 to 4 percent were to be identified within approximately eight weeks.

Binghamton appointed an academic task force of faculty and administrators to recommend cuts and reallocations (a comparable task force for business and student affairs was also appointed). SUNY had completed a system review of doctoral programs, and the New York regents were nearing completion of a similar review. The task force recommended cuts, cost-saving reorganizations, and reallocations based on these and internal campus reviews. Some months later, when SUNY campuses were required to plan for even larger possible budget reductions in fiscal year 1977 (on the border of 10 percent), an administrative team met to analyze program quality and potential and to plan program reductions accordingly. The university community was invited to comment on the plan, which was then revised, circulated, and discussed in hearings with representatives of potentially affected areas.

Meanwhile, the Albany campus, despite the shortage of time, decided to undertake a complete evaluation of all academic programs in order to determine which to maintain, terminate, or enhance. A task force dominated by faculty but including administrators and students was appointed to carry out the evaluations.

The task force rated programs according to eleven criteria: quality of faculty, students, library holdings and facilities, centrality, present and projected student demand, demand for graduates, locational advantage, comparative advantage, cost/revenue relationship, and other costs and benefits. Ultimately, the task force recommended that 20 of Albany's 129 degree programs be terminated and 16 percent of the campus's faculty phased out over a two- to four-year period. Tenured faculty were to be given at least eighteen months' notice (Shirley, 1982).

As in New York, the state of Washington suffered financial reversals that led to five budget reductions at the University of Washington between 1980 and 1982 (Thompson, 1983). Thompson reports that the university had undertaken a series of general program reviews in 1979 in order to acquaint its new president with the university's offerings. As the state's financial situation worsened, these informal efforts grew into a formal "university review" process intended not only to respond to budget reductions but also to scale down and strengthen an "overextended" university.

The University of Minnesota, too, was responding to an anticipated state budget shortfall when it developed a 1981–1983 biennial budget outlining cuts of 12 percent (Heydinger, n.d.). Two years earlier, the university had established a program planning process designed to identify program priorities and integrate them with the budget process. Deans and directors were instructed to plan necessary budget cuts based on the program planning their units had already undertaken. The criteria on which planning had been based included quality; connectedness with other programs; the program's integration of teaching, research, and public service; uniqueness; demand; and cost-effectiveness.

Common Themes—Reallocation Through Program Review. While the details of Binghamton's, Albany's, Washington's, and Minnesota's approaches to reallocation through program review vary, certain common themes are also evident. First, all four institutions were reacting to severe actual or threatened budget shortfalls. Faculty and administrators generally agreed that across-the-board reductions of the required 4 to 12 percent would damage strong, essential programs irreparably. Selective decrements were seen as unavoidable.

To some degree, all four universities had program review processes in place at the time the financial crisis struck. While Albany was at the initiation stage, Binghamton had already established a "priorities committee," and both campuses were involved in statewide doctoral program review efforts by SUNY and the New York State Board of Regents. Washington and Minnesota, both interested in tying program planning to budgets, had worked to implement program review processes. These processes and, perhaps as important, the atmosphere of selectivity and priority setting they encouraged, helped prepare all four universities for the difficult choices to be made.

While administrators made the final reallocation decisions, faculty were heavily involved in the priority-setting process. At Minnesota, the criteria by which programs were ranked were established jointly by the vice-president for academic affairs and a faculty-student governance committee. Once the criteria were specified, faculty established actual program priorities. Washington's administration worked with the faculty senate and a series of administrative-student-faculty committees to develop responses to budget shortfalls. The Albany group that evaluated the campus's programs and recommended program terminations and faculty phase-out consisted of eleven faculty, two administrators, and two students. The academic task force at Binghamton that was asked to recommend reductions of $1.5 million had significant faculty representation. In most instances, faculty of these institutions worked to establish program review criteria and priorities and reacted to administrative reallocation proposals. Only at Albany did a reallocation committee that included faculty recommend substantial faculty terminations.

Finally, while institutions often despair of making judgments about program priorities or suggest that such judgments can be reached only after years of study, the experience of these universities suggests otherwise. Doubtless all wish they had had more time to do their work, but these institutions very quickly selected criteria to be used to establish program priorities, and then assessed adherence to the criteria. Establishing program priorities may well be the sort of task that fills whatever time is allotted to it.

Reduction and Reallocation Experience: Context and Means

The preceding findings from our review of secondary literature can now be supplemented by ten observations about budgeting and resource allocation that have emerged from the site visits conducted for the Project on Reallocation. The literature and the site visits are complementary and, we believe, reinforcing.

The ten observations are clustered around three major headings. The first three points have to do with the context of budget cuts and their impact on institutional politics. The next six point to the strengths and weaknesses of the various reduction and reallocation devices we have observed. Point ten is a comment on consultation processes in reallocation.

Context and Impact of Budget Cuts.

1. There is significant tension between academic and nonacademic areas in resource reallocation.

One large university reported that it had reallocated some $25 million over an eight-year period, but fifteen of that had come from nonacademic areas. Twenty-two of that amount went to pay energy-related bills.

One-third of the chief academic officers responding to our survey reported that money had been allocated *into* academic affairs from other areas during the last three to five years. Forty-seven percent reported no change, and 17 percent reported they had lost money to other areas in the university.

2. Budget cuts and reallocation put great pressure on existing data, formula, and traditional systems of resource allocation.

In one state, the legislators mandated that specified amounts of the projected budgetary cuts come from the administration—in excess of those that otherwise would have been determined by the formula. These cuts were to come specifically out of the system-level office.

In one of our site visits, an associate vice-president had developed an historical measure of student-faculty ratios. The imminent budget reductions put increasing pressure on the ratio since it was based on historical patterns, rather than on a more "rational" analysis of the educational needs of various academic departments. The formula had the effect of grandfathering in what a number of faculty thought were excessively favorable ratios in areas like educational psychology and music. In working out an equitable reduction strategy, these historical student-faculty ratios were attacked, and great pressure was put on the "low" departments to get their ratios up to an acceptable university-wide standard.

Another example of the pressure on data occurred in institutions engaged in decremental strategies. It is very difficult to hand out budget cuts based on *anticipated* enrollment declines. Enrollment projections for individual academic units tend to be an art rather than a science for most institutions. It becomes a "Kentucky-Windage factor" of the highest order to hand out internal budgetary cuts based on projected enrollment declines by academic unit, unless enrollments are capped as a matter of strategic priority rather than as predictions of student demand.

3. Budget cuts and reallocation encourage the "losers" to bypass the system and go to the public, trustees, legislators, and the president.

You have no friends when you cut the budget. Those who are losing funds and resources will never think it fair. For example, most deans of education are committed to healthy schools of education and believe it is lack of wisdom that causes administrators to put pressure on them merely because enrollments are waning. Under systems of strategic choice, it is difficult to persuade the low-priority areas that they should be low priorities.

On the other hand, since a major share of the reallocated money goes to pay the "hidden costs" of energy and fringe benefits, those associated with programs which are identified as high priorities want to know where all the money went! It is probable that funds cannot be reallocated fast enough to handle the shifts in enrollments that occur when students change their preference patterns. Built-in rigidities in the faculty personnel system, for example, work against rapid redeployment of faculty resources into areas that experience marked gains in enrollment over a short (two- to three-year) period of time.

Strengths and Weaknesses of Reduction and Reallocation Devices.
4. Decremental budgets and planning systems help focus attention on priorities.
5. But, unless combined with other than fiscal targets, they are very difficult to implement over time.

One of our cases provides a good example of some of the strengths and weaknesses of the decremental approach to resource reallocation and reduction. The reallocation target system as it evolved at this institution had several elements including:

- Permanent five-year assessments or targets
- Temporary annual targets
- A chief academic officers' revolving fund
- A fund for academic excellence (mostly foundation money)
- A matching equipment fund
- An academic teaching/work-load reserve

The principal comments here are directed towards the permanent five-year targets since the other elements are smaller in amount and result from special monies and identified needs that are independent of academic units.

Each academic unit was put on a five-year decremental target with the average target being 7 percent but the range being from 0 to approximately 15 percent. Planning documents had to be filed as to how the five-year decrement was to be handled in each of approximately twelve academic and ten administrative units.

We concluded that some very good things emerged from these targets. First, the university community now knows that budget shortfalls are reality. Establishing credibility for decrements is one of the principal requisites of an effective system, and the five-year process seemed to do that for this institution.

Second, deans and other academic officers have begun to think of ways of raising money instead of only ways to spend it. The university has conducted workshops for academic leaders to increase their sophistication about how to raise private money. The university has adopted the attitude that requests for "new money" ought to be somehow matched from academic units as well as from institutional funds.

Third, the debate arising from decremental targets has identified at least fourteen major policy dilemmas for university-wide as opposed to college-level decisions. These include enrollment management policies, a university policy on computers, and funding for the libraries.

Fourth, there were several indications that deans and other academic officers were beginning to think about or were actually making vertical as well as horizontal cuts. In other words, they were moving from management by attrition to a more comprehensive attitude about making "choices" based on some rationale other than attrition.

The way in which this institution managed the decrements is crucial to how effective it was over the three- to five-year period under scrutiny. The targets were exclusively in dollars rather than personnel; this caused three problems. First, fiscal targets required the university to announce their decisions about academic areas that would take effect five years in the future. This "prior notice" allowed the opponents of these decisions years to mount opposition and bring political forces to bear against the cuts. How effective this political opposition was would require more detailed treatment than we offer here.

It is important to recognize, however, that political opposition is a significant inhibiting factor in resource allocation decisions. For example, in one case, the collective-bargaining process almost forced the institution to announce faculty layoffs so that "reasonable" contract settlements could be made in exchange for canceling the layoffs. In another institution, the administration had to retract a series of program reduction decisions for political rather than academic or financial reasons.

Second, the data base was not sophisticated enough to allow the making of decisions five years in advance. For example, the enrollment situation in one of the academic units was the rationale used for budget cuts, yet that academic unit improved its enrollment situation two or three years into the budget cycle. The institution was forced to come up with a way to "relieve" some of the target.

Third, the target system was inflexible in that it did not allow the central administration to capture at least some of the benefits of serendipity. The flexibility gained when faculty leave, retire early, or die accrued to the academic units, not to central administration.

    6. Reallocation decisions should be made by the next highest level because it involves setting relative priorities among academic units.

One of the major internal debates about reallocation is the relative authority of various levels in the decision-making structure. Private institutions who operate on fiscal philosophies of "every tub on its own bottom" have to resolve the dilemma of how much of the total institutional revenue of the institution belongs to the university as opposed to the subunit that generates it. One private university has decided that it will use most of its income from annual giving to "subsidize" the liberal arts college. The professional schools are supposed to be on a "break-even" basis. Public institutions that get state funds on a formula basis find it difficult to reallocate internal funds using some method other than the formula.

The point here is that it requires leadership of the highest order to establish that setting priorities among academic units is the responsibility of the next highest level of decision making.

    7. The strategy of "starving the problems and feeding the opportunities" (SPFO) requires a consistent definition of problems and opportunities.

Since most reallocation we have observed is on the margins—on the order of 1 or 2 percent per year—it normally takes three to five years before there is a significant impact. The most common problem with such a time frame is the "zigzag effect"—that is, this year's problems turn into next year's opportunities, and this year's opportunities become next year's problems. This may be due to shifting enrollment patterns, a change in the leadership of the institution or some of the academic units involved, or as a result of some of the political pressures and personalities mentioned earlier.

Where such factors are substantial, the net effect of a reallocation scheme over a period of five years may be zero.

8. The key to success in strategic choice is modest expectations.

Strategic planning and budgeting systems, funds for academic excellence, and priority decision making are often sold as the principal, if not only, route to academic survival and excellence. In the last five to ten years, many of these schemes have been successful in finding funds for paying increased energy and fringe-benefit costs. These are monies that are not visible to those deans that have experienced rapid enrollment increases, and they legitimately ask, "What happened to all the money?" They seldom support these systems because they do not see the evidence that they are effective—that is, they do not see increased resources allocated into their areas. They often are supported in their dismay by professional accreditation agencies who argue that increased resources are needed in order to maintain accreditation.

If higher education continues its overwhelming pattern of allocating resources based on *gradual* incremental or decremental patterns, one can be reasonably skeptical of devices that promise to remake such historical truths.

9. Administrative reorganization and program closures do not save tangible money in the short run, *unless people are terminated.*

Since most of the costs of programs are in the people used to staff them, cost savings without terminations are unlikely. On the other hand, program closures and reorganizations may save funds over the long run through effective management by attrition (Dougherty, 1981).

Consultation in Resource Reallocation

10. Faculty committees work best when they are not asked about individual programs or people but about methods and criteria.

The academic community requires that faculty be consulted about such important decisions as program reductions and closure as well as, in some cases, reallocation plans. Many faculty refuse to participate in the identification of which colleagues will be terminated. In some cases, they are willing to participate in the identification of programs to be closed, but only after extensive debate about the method, process, and criteria being used to arrive at such judgments.

In the secondary literature identified, there are several examples where faculty committees have operated effectively in arriving at criteria for resource reallocation. For example, the University of Washington Faculty Senate passed a policy on criteria for resource reallocation.

Many times faculty senates and committees support the need to close programs. They breathe a collective sigh of relief when "marginal" programs are identified as targets for closure.

In a small liberal arts college (one of our site visits), the chief academic officer provided information and analysis for a faculty committee. The committee eventually supported his judgment that closures and terminations were necessary, but the committee refused to identify the specific individuals or programs to be terminated. Yet the legitimacy gained by this extensive consultation was a crucial ingredient in maintaining civility on campus during the terminations.

In another case, a standing committee of the faculty senate—the layoff committee—was successful in persuading the administration that layoffs were not necessary if certain other reallocation policies and practices were adopted. This faculty committee was very active in persuading colleagues in departments around the university to get their teaching loads and student-faculty ratios more in line with university-wide criteria.

In still another case, a university created a budget panel consisting of administrators and faculty. This panel advised the administration annually concerning resource allocation on campus. The administration's deliberations in times of budget cuts were also aided by a rather comprehensive backlog of program reviews. These reviews became an important source of information for the budget panel and in the eventual identification of areas for budget cuts.

A Concluding Note: A Holistic View

This chapter has concentrated on resource reallocation and reduction and ignored the other elements that would be involved in a more comprehensive view of the way institutions deal with scarcity and environmental uncertainty. There are four sets of policies necessary to develop this holistic view:
- Enrollment management policies that deal both with institutional and subinstitutional levels.
- Personnel policies that are linked with
- Fiscal and
- Programmatic decisions.

The Project on Reallocation will speak to these linkages in a more comprehensive way in subsequent publications.

References

Balderston, F. E. *Managing Today's University.* San Francisco: Jossey-Bass, 1974.
Bowen, F. M., and Glenny, L. A. *State Budgeting for Higher Education: State*

Fiscal Stringency and Public Education. Berkeley: Center for Research and Development in Higher Education, University of California, 1976.

Bowen, F. M., and Glenny, L. A. "The California Study." In L. Leslie and J. Hyatt (Eds.), *Higher Education Financing Policies: States/Institutions and Their Interactions.* Tucson: Center for the Study of Higher Education, University of Arizona, 1981.

Dickmeyer, N. *Financial Conditions of Colleges and Universities.* Washington, D.C.: American Council on Education and National Association of College and University Business Officers, 1983.

Dougherty, E. A. "Evaluating and Discontinuing Programs." In J. R. Mingle and Associates (Eds.), *Challenges of Retrenchment: Strategies for Consolidating Programs, Cutting Costs, and Reallocating Resources.* San Francisco: Jossey-Bass, 1981.

Fortunato, R. J., and Waddell, D. G. *Personnel Administration in Higher Education: Handbook of Faculty and Staff Personnel Practices.* San Francisco: Jossey-Bass, 1981.

Furman, J. "State Budgeting and Retrenchment." In J. R. Mingle and Associates (Eds.), *Challenges of Retrenchment: Strategies for Consolidating Programs, Cutting Costs, and Reallocating Resources.* San Francisco: Jossey-Bass, 1981.

Glenny, L. A. "The Concept of Short-Run Decision Making." In R. Wilson (Ed.), *Responses to Fiscal Stress in Higher Education.* Tucson: Center for the Study of Higher Education, University of Arizona, 1982.

Gray, J. A. "Legal Restraints on Faculty Cutbacks." In J. R. Mingle and Associates (Eds.), *Challenges of Retrenchment: Strategies for Consolidating Programs, Cutting Costs, and Reallocating Resources.* San Francisco: Jossey-Bass, 1981.

Hammond, M., and Tompkins, L. D. "A Major University's Response to a Mandated Budget Recision." Paper presented at the annual meeting of the Association for the Study of Higher Education, Washington, D.C., March 25, 1983.

Heydinger, R. B. *Using Program Priorities to Make Retrenchment Decisions: The Case of the University of Minnesota.* Atlanta: Southern Regional Education Board, no date.

Hruby, N. J. *A Survival Kit for Invisible Colleges: What to Do until Federal Aid Arrives.* Washington, D.C.: Management Division, Academy for Educational Development, 1973.

Ihrig, W. E. "Resource Reallocations at the Ohio State University." In R. Wilson (Ed.), *Survival in the 1980s: Quality, Mission, and Financing Options.* Tucson: Center for the Study of Higher Education, University of Arizona, 1983.

Jedamus, P. "Legislative Action: The Possibility of Instant Retrenchment." *Journal of the College and University Personnel Association,* 1980, *31,* 38-46.

Johnson, M. D., and Mortimer, K. P. *Faculty Bargaining and the Politics of Retrenchment in the Pennsylvania State Colleges, 1971-1976.* University Park: Center for the Study of Higher Education, University of Pennsylvania 1977.

Johnstone, W. A. "Faculty Retrenchment in the 1980s: A Question of How Many? and How Managed?" *Journal of the College and University Personnel Association,* 1980, *31,* 22-30.

Kreinin, M. E. "Preserving Tenure Commitments in Hard Times: The Michigan State Experience." *Academe,* 1982, *68* (2), 7-15, 37-45.

La Tourette, J. E. "The SUNY-Binghamton Experience with Retrenchment, 1975-76." Unpublished manuscript, no date.

Lee, J. *Case Studies of Institutions in Decline.* Washington, D.C.: National Institute of Education, 1981.

Lozier, G. G., and Althouse, P. R. "Developing Planning and Budgeting Strategies for Internal Recycling of Funds." *Research in Higher Education*, 1983, *18*, 237-250.

Melchiori, G. S. "Smaller and Better: The University of Michigan Experience." *Research in Higher Education*, 1982, *16*, 55-69.

Millington, P. "An Institutional Perspective: Stanford." In L. Leslie and J. Hyatt (Eds.), *Higher Education Financing Policies: States/Institutions and Their Interactions*. Tucson: Center for the Study of Higher Education, University of Arizona, 1981.

Mingle, J. R. "Redirecting Higher Education in a Time of Budget Reduction." *Issues in Higher Education*, no. 18. Atlanta: Southern Regional Education Board, 1982.

Minter, J. W., and Bowen, H. R. "Despite Economic Ills, Colleges Weathered the 70s with Larger Enrollments and Stronger Programs." *Chronicle of Higher Education*, May 12, 1982, pp. 5-7.

Mortimer, K. P. "Procedures and Criteria for Faculty Retrenchment." In J. R. Mingle and Associates (Eds.), *Challenges of Retrenchment: Strategies for Consolidating Programs, Cutting Costs, and Reallocating Resources*. San Francisco: Jossey-Bass, 1981.

Mortimer, K. P., and Tierney, M. *The Three R's of the Eighties: Reduction, Reallocation, and Retrenchment*. AAHE-ERIC/Higher Education Report No. 4. Washington, D.C.: American Association for Higher Education, 1979.

Otzenberger, S. J., and Kaelke, M. E. "The MSU Scenario: A Basis for Discussion." *Journal of the College and University Personnel Association*, 1980, *31*, 1-6.

Robl, R. K., Karman, T. A., and Boggs, J. H. "Quality and Vitality Through Reallocation: A Case History." *Planning for Higher Education*, 1976, *5*, 1-7.

Shirley, R. C. "The SUNY-Albany Experience." In R. Wilson (Ed.), *Responses to Fiscal Stress in Higher Education*. Tucson: Center for the Study of Higher Education, University of Arizona, 1982.

Stadtman, V. A. *Academic Adaptations: Higher Education Prepares for the 1980s and 1990s*. San Francisco: Jossey-Bass, 1980.

Thompson, R. K. "Maintaining Quality Programs During Periods of Financial Stress." In R. Wilson (Ed.), *Survival in the 1980s: Quality, Mission, and Financing Options*. Tucson: Center for the Study of Higher Education, University of Arizona, 1983.

Kenneth P. Mortimer is a professor of higher education and director of the Project on Reallocation at The Pennsylvania State University.

Barbara E. Taylor is assistant to the vice-chancellor for policy programs and planning at State University of New York.

The previous chapters provide a broad and integrated treatment of the new financing strategies.

Bringing the Issues Together

Larry L. Leslie

Synthesis

The previous four chapters systematically have examined recent developments in funding and budgeting strategies. This chapter synthesizes the previous four, fills gaps they leave in the topic of new financing strategies, and suggests sources of additional information.

Chapter One. The first chapter provides a roadmap of where we have been and of the alternative routes to where we are going, and it is highly successful in offering a clear analysis of the options. As new courses of action are considered, a central task of institutional research is to help other decision makers understand the underlying principles—or "root forces," as Morgan calls them—of these alternatives.

Morgan lays out two general theories of resource allocation and describes what each has to offer. He takes our eye off the hundreds of distracting details concerning each specific strategy and focuses our attention on the most fundamental issue—the principles upon which the strategies are presumed to work. In an area where advocates of new strategies can possess the righteous zeal of a fundamentalist preacher and the persuasiveness of an old time flimflam man, this guidance is badly needed. Morgan is telling us to be aware of what we are buying; if we understand the principles upon which an innovation is based, then our decisions can be made astutely.

What Morgan demonstrates once again is that there is never anything completely new—although the variations in the old may be quite important. Essentially, the choice in budgeting strategies is between those that optimize the fundamental tenets of modern management science—effectiveness and efficiency—and those that complement the realities of organizational political environments. His conclusion, which may benefit from elaboration here, is that strategies that draw upon the strengths of both models, if carefully orchestrated, may enjoy the major advantages of each while overcoming many of the serious liabilities.

A central aspect of Morgan's market interaction model is the interplay of interest groups in determining final solutions. The decision-making environment may be conceptualized as a Lewinian field in which individuals and groups interact to influence decisions that concern them. Each is motivated heavily by enlightened self-interest. Think, for example, of the competition among college deans, vice-presidents, and directors of independent units within a complex university as annual resource allocations are made. A more concise example might be the interactions of actors in the annual state budgetary process, where agency heads (such as college presidents, prison wardens, the state public school superintendent, and the welfare director) compete for scarce resources from the legislature, and the legislature, in turn, is attempting to reconcile pressures from the governor with those from taxpayer groups and special-interest lobbies and with some sense of what the voters really want. Or consider the interplay of actors within an academic or administrative subunit of a college or university as resources are further allocated to unit budgets and final objects of expenditure.

By using this vertical extension of examples, one can illustrate some differences in how each of Morgan's two models might work, independently or jointly. Clearly, the state-level example suggests most strongly the appropriateness of the market interaction model since the environment is classically political. That is, for one to enjoy "success" on the state level, strategies employed must reflect the realities of the political game. An agency head, such as a college president, might well enhance the institutional budget through demonstration of the rational aspects of resource utilization and needs assessment, but successful tactics chosen for legislative interface will also be heavily political. This is because the rules of the game center upon the legislator's needs, which reflect political reward and punishment.

On the other hand, as one moves down the organizational structure, elements of the rational calculation model will prove more useful because incentive systems tend to become less political and more rational—as Morgan uses the terms. (The separation point is probably the campus president, who occupies the no-man's land between the two separate value and decision systems.) In comparison to prevailing principles in most other kinds of organizations, colleges or universities place an unusually high value on rational strategies.

This is not to say that the market interaction or political model is irrelevant within the college or university. The distinction made here is one of degrees. The experienced collegiate administrator knows that political behaviors are commonplace within academic settings.

Nevertheless, most so-called innovative approaches to resource allocation and budgeting in higher education are based upon the rational model; as Morgan notes, "market interaction assumptions tend to be less prevalent." This reflects not only the academic value system but also the role assigned by society to the professional, such as the institutional researcher or budget officer. His or her role is to develop and advocate the rational solution, both within the organization and within the political arena. Indeed, the common implicit and often explicit task assigned to institutional administrators, or at least assumed by them, is to find ways (rational ways) to overcome political tendencies—that is, to prevent political decisions from occurring. The role of the political decision maker, on the other hand, be he or she a campus leader or an elected leader, is to balance the rationally ideal with political realities. In this sense, the classical tests of rationality, effectiveness and efficiency, become subcomponents of the political or market interaction model. (For such a model applied to specific higher education issues, see Leslie, 1976; 1980.)

As Morgan proposes, superior institutional solutions will reflect a synthesis of the two models. The discussion here suggests that successful new strategies for resource allocation and budgeting will be heavily rational but also will be realistic in the political sense. Such strategies will require a constant search for more effective techniques that are both manageable within the constraints of institutional capabilities and feasible in the political arena.

Chapter Two. This chapter causes one to reconsider the statement that nothing is ever really new, since there is so much going on in the formula budgeting area. Brinkman has collected in one brief chapter all that is noteworthy in the existing literature in regard to the allocation formula as a public policy device and to what is new in formula design and implementation.

According to Morgan, the formula is one of the many "rational calculation" techniques that has arrived on the higher education financing scene in recent decades. Brinkman demonstrates that the present thrust in regard to formulas is in refining existing formula approaches, designing means of solving inherent problems, and, as he puts it, in overcoming formula "tendencies."

This distinction is an important one. Brinkman is saying that formulas have intrinsic properties that seem to be accompanied by undesirable side effects. He does not seem to see these so much as flaws as necessary outgrowths of a highly bureaucratic technique. In this he is almost too fair-minded.

For formulas to achieve their stated potentials, certain difficulties must arise. For example, the quantitative orientation of formulas must lead to a denigration of the qualitative; attention to equity must lead to leveling and loss of diversity within a state system. States can indeed seek to ameliorate these problems, as have Kentucky and Minnesota, if they are willing to trade off some of the intrinsic advantages of formulas. However, the unavoidable result must be a reduction in the emphasis placed on formulas and increased emphasis on alternative strategies. A reading of the Kentucky, Minnesota, and other state changes might be described as movement away from formulas to a more balanced position between formulas and other less rational techniques. That is, if formulas are, as Miller's (1964) benchmark definition suggests, "an objective procedure for estimating the further budgetary requirements of a college or university," then provisions for funding special activities, management incentives, enrollment buffers, and the like must be departures from formulas.

Most formula adaptations or deviations reflect Morgan's recommendation that the highly rational financial technique be balanced with elements of the market interaction model. Perhaps this is inevitable. At an invited seminar of national finance experts recently, there seemed to emerge a clear consensus that formulas ultimately become highly politicized. Indeed, the view was espoused that formulas are just another form by which political consensus may be expressed; that is, the elements of formulas are little more than expressions of political agreements—they represent the equilibrium among competing political forces.

This seems to go a bit far. It is true that those with experience with formulas can point to numerous cases of how formulas have been changed to reflect political considerations. For example, it is common (if not standard) practice, before any formula changes are formalized, to check the allocative effects to state institutions of revised formulas against the shares realized by each institution under the old formula. This is the classical "fair shares" consideration of the political process (Wildavsky, 1974). (Note also Brinkman's reference to fair shares as a *strength* of formulas.) Yet formulas originally evolved in order to reduce political logrolling, and they do achieve this end. Recent changes, then, seem to represent a readjustment in the balance between political and apolitical forces. Or perhaps Jones (forthcoming) makes the more insightful comment when he observes that, where formulas are concerned, the politics are taken care of before the formula is adopted. This view satisfies both camps: State political leaders are allowed to have their turn in satisfying interest groups, and professional administrators can feel that rational objectives were met too.

It is noteworthy that at the top of Brinkman's list of inherent formula problems or tendencies are those that reflect insensitivity to the political process. The "cures" noted in Kentucky and Minnesota are attempts to redress some of the past imbalance toward the rational and away from the political. For example (as noted in Chapter Two), in achieving objectivity through quantitative focus, formulas have created a distinct pattern of incentives, and institutions, as good rationalistic actors, have changed their behaviors accordingly. But the incentives have sometimes been misplaced and qualitative goals have been shorted. With changing public priorities and concerns vis-à-vis higher education (such as the current focus on quality), formulas become at best inadequate and at worst dysfunctional. Formulas depoliticized higher education financing; a partial return to political considerations now is needed. Demands for public accountability in regard to important higher education issues are direct manifestations of this need. Society does not wish to leave important issues such as quality achievement to chance, and public institutions may not ignore societal wishes.

Finally, something more might be said in relation to the role of costing in establishing the specific quantitative elements of formulas. When formulas are viewed as classically defined in Chapter Two—as opposed to the broader interpretations of Kentucky and Minnesota—some form of cost calculation must be used, whether it be from a periodic in-state costing study or from studies in other selected states. Thus, a discussion of formulas could concern itself solely with costing.

As Brinkman notes, the connection between costing and formulas usually renders the latter a conservative or status quo device. Historic costs invariably drive funding formulas. Hence, costs and formulas are normative. This year's formula reflects last year's cost patterns in state institutions or, infrequently, such as in Kentucky, patterns in other states. In short, formulas base their allocations upon the allocations of the past. Usually the past allocation is used to validate new formulas.

Chapter Three. Allen lays out five incentive financing models that cut across Morgan's two basic categories of the rational analytical and the market interaction. Morgan, however, labels incentives structures as only market interaction devices because incentives, he believes, are intended to induce marketplace behaviors. Allen implies a broader definition of incentives by observing indirectly that any financing structure contains both incentives and disincentives. Any connection of appropriations or allocations to specific behaviors, events, or occurrences will elicit responses from subordinate units and their subunits. To Allen, the rewarded behaviors, events, or occurrences demonstrate incentives; the unrewarded represent disincentives.

Viewed in this way, forced compliance or controls exercised by a central organization, such as a state governing board or a campus central administration, become negative incentives (punishment) to subordinate units (Allen's model one). The incentive is to do what one is told if one wishes to avoid personal or organizational punishment. Model two also reflects Allen's liberal definition. Here, the elements upon which state allocation formulas are based are viewed as the incentives. Institutions, for example, are provided incentives to enroll students, reclassify courses as upper division or graduate, reclassify students as vocational, or relabel remedial courses as college level. They may experience disincentives to provide student services, improve instruction, or offer courses in low-demand fields.

Morgan's framework would classify Allen's first two models as rational; market interaction requires more in the way of negotiation of strategies and goals and less in the way of the objective goal-based tests of effectiveness and efficiency characteristic of rational management.

The third model, too, would be considered a rational device in Morgan's terms. Outcomes budgeting is performance budgeting in which funds follow specific achievements or productions. No system could fit the rational model better. By definition, effectiveness *is* goal achievement.

Only models four and five clearly fit Morgan's classification of incentives because only in these are give and take inherent—that is, the interactions of the market. In model four, the distinction between the rational and the market models becomes clear. Good management practices are rewarded, as in the case of student follow-ups, but interaction and negotiation, the traits of the marketplace, are required to define what good management practice is. More important, management is required to take account of client-consumer needs of students. In model five, full-responsibility funding, the incentives and the elements of the market are most in evidence. Prices (tuitions) are set in accordance with supply and demand, competition is carefully evaluated, "profits" in the form of end-of-year balances become all-important in that they are carried forward, products (programs) are altered, new markets are sought, and efforts are targeted upon increasing (positively) the revenue-expenditure gap.

The differing operational definitions of Allen and Morgan are of little real consequence. Literally, each of Allen's five models illustrates incentives; however, since our topic here is new financing strategies, a more specific meaning of the term incentives is probably needed. "New" incentives are assumed to be special provisions that reinforce specific actions, rather than any means to routinize financial support (as is the case, for example, in the use of formulas). Incentives generally are add-ons; they are additions to the routine.

Seen as the new, the nonroutine, the add-on, then, incentive financing systems are scarce. A large reason may be that, anomalously, the market interaction model, though akin to the political model, possesses political liabilities. For example, the Endowed Teachers and Scholars Program in Texas violates fundamental political tenets such as equity and fair shares. Presumably, the program can survive and flourish in Texas because the University of Texas system has statewide political support. One might suspect, however, that communities containing public colleges not a part of the University of Texas would be less enthusiastic about this program.

The Colorado approach to incentive financing would seem to be on even shakier political ground. Normally, strong public accountability is demanded for any significant public expenditure. Although, under the Memorandum of Understanding (MOU), the state maintains some direct checks and controls on higher education, accountability is relatively very modest. The new Colorado financing system evolved at a time when state resources were the scarcest they had been since the Great Depression. In the political process, extreme circumstances often lead to extreme solutions; resistance to dramatic change is never weaker. Yet one must wonder what will happen when normal financial times return to the state. Will the body politic tolerate higher and higher tuitions, limited places for in-state students, and market-type behaviors by tax-supported institutions? The budget surplus at the University of Colorado-Boulder has been the first test; the margin by which the MOU survived apparently was small. One suspects that Colorado universities continually will be called upon to reconfirm the advantages of the new financing system to the public, either in the form of demonstrated reduced costs, improved quality, or both.

Chapter Four. This chapter cuts across the previous ones by examining finance-related activities within institutions. Whereas Chapters Two and Three discuss specific new financing strategies, including vertical applications of these single strategies, Chapter Four goes inside the institutions to see what forms of financial adjustment are being employed and what the effects may be. Here the world does not appear so highly ordered.

This is the nature of reality. Planners and policy makers lay out their schemes in crisp terms and in a highly logical order; deployment often more closely resembles a battlefield.

Mortimer and Taylor bring considerable order to the apparent disarray by organizing events, decisions, and directions into several categories. The viewing of financial reactions during periods of decline as reallocation, reduction in size, and retrenchment is a useful division. These three types of response reflect important differences in management philosophy, financial condition, and institutional impact.

The categorizations and treatment of the middle section of the chapter are likewise insightful. The aggregation of across-the-board versus selective strategies is a common approach to managing the analysis of financial adjustment; however, distinctions made between such subcategories as across-the-board attrition versus across-the-board decrements offer new conceptual assistance to the financial manager. There are several alternative tools within the across-the-board or selective arsenal, each of which is not necessarily a separate blunt instrument. Further, each separate tool possesses both positive potentials and liabilities.

Yet perhaps the most useful, and certainly the most interesting, part of the discussion is in the final third of the chapter, in which institutional cases are treated directly. Here the strategies come to life and the ten themes offered abound with useful ideas for financial management. This section allows us to spot where our own institutions went wrong, or occasionally right, and where a pitfall may be avoided in the future.

Finally, in looking at Chapter Four, we find that Morgan's framework once again proves its worth. Institutional events reflect the fundamental dichotomy described by Morgan, as well as the role of the professional in all of this. The bias of Mortimer and Taylor, as befits the professional manager/analyst, is rationalistic. The authors' assessments are based upon rational tests and rational assumptions. Political logrolling enters the discussion primarily in the form of obstructions to be overcome.

Had Mortimer and Taylor seen Morgan's chapter before designing their study, they might have added an extra element to their data gathering. One could hypothesize a theory of institutional response to fiscal stress from Morgan's work and test that theory with time-series data. Such an attempt was made using the Bowen-Glenny data collected in California (Leslie, 1983). Bowen and Glenny's five sequential stages of reactions to fiscal stress were placed on a continuum that utilized "reactivity" as the defining concept. The pattern obtained was clear-cut. In early stages of decline, institutional actions are highly political; above all they seem to be aimed at keeping interest-group reactivity at a low level. However, as fiscal conditions worsen, more traditionally rational approaches begin to appear and, by the time the crisis truly arrives, rational strategies of high reactivity are commonplace. It seems clear that highly rational reactive strategies become politically feasible when conditions become desperate, but not much before.

Filling the Gaps

The strategy used in organizing this volume was to follow a framework chapter with a thorough discussion of the two topics that encompass most new financing approaches. In a sense, the fourth chapter rotated the analysis by ninety degrees and reported on institutional cases. Few important gaps remain.

If we refer once again to Morgan's Figure 1, the one financing innovation that demands additional discussion is responsibility-center budgeting. In this approach, each university academic subunit, usually the college or division, is relatively autonomous financially. After assessments for general administration and related activities are made, all remaining unit revenues are assigned to the unit, and, with previously specified exceptions, expenditures must be made within these revenue constraints. Ordinarily, a transition period is provided to allow each unit time to become self-sufficient, and financial planning/decision cycles extend beyond a single year.

Responsibility-center budgeting is the ultimate in accountability and at first glance appears to be overwhelmingly rational. What could be more rational than directly connecting revenues and expenditures? The problem, of course, is that effectiveness—the accomplishment of goals—is not synonymous with accountability in a complex organization. Academic units are not independent. True, their faculties may rarely interact directly, but student and curricular interactions are widespread. Various curricular models allocate general and liberal education courses in various ways—some concentrate such courses in the first two years of the bachelor's degree program while others integrate them throughout entire student programs. Then there are the associated or closely allied courses, (often service courses) that also may be concentrated in time or may be integrated. Examples are mathematics, chemistry, and physics courses for engineers; political and sociological theory courses for public administrators; and philosophy, theology, and psychology courses in contemporary allied health programs. The elements of the production function of higher education extend beyond artificial unit boundaries.

It is in the allocation decision rules that the political logrolling occurs, and market interaction extends beyond the agreement events. The problems here are very similar to those of program budgeting, in which deliberation over credit for service and other courses must be conducted and units must decide whether to offer such courses, change their own curricula so as to capture additional resources, and engage in trading faculty time.

Units must also respond heavily to the form of incentives offered. Usually, the incentives are in the instructional area, to the detriment of research and public service activities. Resource sharing for interunit projects of all kinds often is subject to the negotiation of sharing units.

Responsibility-center budgeting has great rational appeal at a time of rapidly shifting enrollments within institutions. Internal political principles such as incrementalism and fair shares mitigate strongly against rapid resource reallocation as student demand for separate units ebbs and flows. Responsibility-center budgeting, at least in theory, moves resources around in near-direct correspondence with enrollments—

toward business and computer science departments, at present, and away from education and the liberal arts.

Responsibility-center budgeting is described more fully in references cited in Chapter One. The approach has been used predominantly, if not exclusively, in private universities. Harvard, the University of Pennsylvania, and Vanderbilt are well-known examples.

Sources of Additional Assistance

The general topic of coping with the financial problems being encountered and those anticipated in higher education in this decade has been the focus of annual conferences conducted at the University of Arizona since the late 1970s. Papers from these conferences have been published annually in conference proceedings as follows:

Harcleroad, F. F. (Ed.). *Financing Postsecondary Education in the 1980s.* Tucson: Center for the Study of Higher Education, University of Arizona, 1979.
Leslie, L. L., and Otto, H. L. (Eds.). *Financing and Budgeting Postsecondary Education in the 1980s.* Tucson: Center for the Study of Higher Education, University of Arizona, 1980.
Leslie, L. L., and Hyatt, J. (Eds.). *Higher Education Financing Policies: States/Institutions and Their Interactions.* Tucson: Center for the Study of Higher Education, University of Arizona, 1981.
Wilson, R. A. (Ed.). *Responses to Fiscal Stress in Higher Education.* Tucson: Center for the Study of Higher Education, University of Arizona, 1982.
Wilson, R. A. (Ed.). *Survival in the 1980s: Quality, Mission, and Financing Options.* Tucson: Center for the Study of Higher Education, University of Arizona, 1983.

These volumes contain papers that speak to all aspects of new financing strategies, from their conceptual frameworks to institutional case studies. Conceptual papers include the following:

Andringa, R. C. "The Political-Economic Context for Financing Postsecondary Education in the 1980s." In L. L. Leslie and H. L. Otto (Eds.), *Financing and Budgeting Postsecondary Education in the 1980s.* Tucson: Center for the Study of Higher Education, University of Arizona, 1980.
Bennet, R. F. "Financing Postsecondary Education in the '80s: A Governor's Perspective." In F. F. Harcleroad (Ed.), *Financing Postsecondary Education in the 1980s.* Tucson: Center for the Study of Higher Education, University of Arizona, 1979.
Bowen, H. R. "Unused Capacity: Opportunity or Disaster." In F. F. Harcleroad (Ed.), *Financing Postsecondary Education in the 1980s.* Tucson: Center for the Study of Higher Education, University of Arizona, 1979.
Boyer, E. "Higher Education Financing Policies: A Context." In L. L. Leslie and J. Hyatt (Eds.), *Higher Education Financing Policies: States/Institutions and Their Interactions.* Tucson: Center for the Study of Higher Education, University of Arizona, 1981.

Jones, G. "Reagan Administration Policy Statement on Higher Education Finance." In R. A. Wilson (Ed.), *Responses to Fiscal Stress in Higher Education*. Tucson: Center for the Study of Higher Education, University of Arizona, 1982.

Kerr, C. "Survival in the 1980s." In R. A. Wilson (Ed.), *Survival in the 1980s: Quality, Mission, and Financing Options*. Tucson: Center for the Study of Higher Education, University of Arizona, 1983.

Leslie, L. L. "The Financial Prospects for Higher Education in the '80s." In F. F. Harcleroad (Ed.), *Financing Postsecondary Education in the 1980s*. Tucson: Center for the Study of Higher Education, University of Arizona, 1979.

Wildavsky, A. "Uses of Adversity in Higher Education." In R. A. Wilson (Ed.), *Responses to Fiscal Stress in Higher Education*. Tucson: Center for the Study of Higher Education, University of Arizona, 1982.

Papers that describe state and institutional responses to fiscal stress include the following:

Brown, B. "Information Needs for Budgetary Analysis: The University of Houston Experience." In L. L. Leslie and J. Hyatt (Eds.), *Higher Education Financing Policies: States/Institutions and Their Interactions*. Tucson: Center for the Study of Higher Education, University of Arizona, 1981.

Curry, D. J. "Consequences of Budget Reduction Strategies: The Washington Experience." In R. A. Wilson (Ed.), *Survival in the 1980s: Quality, Mission, and Financing Options*. Tucson: Center for the Study of Higher Education, University of Arizona, 1983.

Hewitt, C. N. "Campus Renewal in the 1980s: The New Voyage of the Beagle." In R. A. Wilson (Ed.), *Responses to Fiscal Stress in Higher Education*. Tucson: Center for the Study of Higher Education, University of Arizona, 1982.

McCoy, M. "Quality and Budget Flexibility: Case Example at the University of Colorado." In R. A. Wilson (Ed.), *Survival in the 1980s: Quality, Mission, and Financing Options*. Tucson: Center for the Study of Higher Education, University of Arizona, 1983.

McKinney, D. L. "The University of Idaho Experience." In R. A. Wilson (Ed.), *Responses to Fiscal Stress in Higher Education*. Tucson: Center for the Study of Higher Education, University of Arizona, 1982.

Millington, P. "An Institutional Perspective: Stanford." In L. L. Leslie and J. Hyatt (Eds.), *Higher Education Financing Policies: States/Institutions and Their Interactions*. Tucson: Center for the Study of Higher Education, University of Arizona, 1981.

Pickens, W., Hyer, G., and Thompson, R. "Managing Fiscal Crisis: The California, Wisconsin, and Washington Experiences." In L. L. Leslie and J. Hyatt (Eds.), *Higher Education Financing Policies: States/Institutions and Their Interactions*. Tucson: Center for the Study of Higher Education, University of Arizona, 1981.

Seitz, C., Schultze, R., and Baughman, G. "Budgeting in Enrollment Decline: The Indiana, Virginia, and Ohio Experiences." In L. L. Leslie and J. Hyatt (Eds.), *Higher Education Financing Policies: States/Institutions and Their Interactions*. Tucson: Center for the Study of Higher Education, University of Arizona, 1981.

Shirley, R. C. "The SUNY-Albany Experience." In R. A. Wilson (Ed.), *Responses to Fiscal Stress in Higher Education*. Tucson: Center for the Study of Higher Education, University of Arizona, 1982.

Whalen, E. "Expected Conditions and Potential Responses." In L. L. Leslie and J. Hyatt (Eds.), *Higher Education Financing Policies: States/Institutions and Their Interactions.* Tucson: Center for the Study of Higher Education, University of Arizona, 1981.

Several papers in these edited works address the specific topics addressed in this sourcebook. For example:

Hartmark, L. S. "A Planning, Budgeting, and Evaluation System: Lessons from Experience." In R. A. Wilson (Ed.), *Survival in the 1980s: Quality, Mission, and Financing Options.* Tucson: Center for the Study of Higher Education, University of Arizona, 1983.
Hyde, W. "Tuition Pricing Policies and Their Effects on Institutions." In R. A. Wilson (Ed.), *Responses to Fiscal Stress in Higher Education.* Tucson: Center for the Study of Higher Education, University of Arizona, 1982.
Millard, R. "Quality Promotion in the Steady State." In L. L. Leslie and H. L. Otto (Eds.), *Financing and Budgeting Postsecondary Education in the 1980s.* Tucson: Center for the Study of Higher Education, University of Arizona, 1980.
Pickens, W. H. "Performance Funding in Higher Education: Panacea or Price?" In R. A. Wilson (Ed.), *Survival in the 1980s: Quality, Mission, and Financing Options.* Tucson: Center for the Study of Higher Education, University of Arizona, 1983.
Siren, R. L. "Strategies Planning in the Small, Private, Liberal Arts Institutions." In R. A. Wilson (Ed.), *Responses to Fiscal Stress in Higher Education.* Tucson: Center for the Study of Higher Education, University of Arizona, 1982.

The reader may also wish to consult:

Mortimer, K. P., and Tierney, M. L. *The Three "R's" of the Eighties: Reduction, Reallocation, and Retrenchment.* Washington: American Association for Higher Education, 1979.

This monograph discusses the demographic environment of the 1980s and trends in the institutional revenues and expenditures. After reductions in salary expenditures, staff positions, and student-faculty ratios are described, means of internal reallocation are addressed, with special attention devoted to program review. The authors use their own research plus published reports in the literature to formulate their generalizations. This volume was a forerunner to Mortimer's Lilly Endowment study.

A thorough treatment of formulas, including recent developments, is combined in the following volume:

Jones, D. *Higher Education Budgeting at the State Level: Formula Funding in Context.* Boulder, Colo.: National Center for Higher Education Management Systems, forthcoming.

Many states have reconsidered their entire postsecondary financing systems. Excellent policy papers, such as those written for the California Postsecondary Education Commission, often have been composed. One may query state councils, commissions, and coordinating and governing boards as to document availability. One excellent example is:

Curry, D. J., Fischer, N. M., and Jons, T. *State Policy Options for Financing Higher Education.* Olympia: State of Washington Council for Postsecondary Education, 1982.

The reader also should consult other *New Directions for Institutional Research* volumes. In recent years numerous issues have addressed topics directly related to the enrollment and financial stress now widespread in American higher education. Although few of these volumes are specifically of a financial nature, almost invariably financing strategies are either at the heart of or are much involved in proposed solutions to management problems. One of the more outstanding examples is:

Heydinger, R. B. (Ed.). *Academic Program Planning for the 1980s.* New Directions for Institutional Research, no. 28. San Francisco: Jossey-Bass, 1980. The chapter by Hoenack and Berg in this volume provides a standard for conceptual and analytical thought on the topic of incentives.

References

Jones, D. P. *Higher Education Budgeting at the State Level: Formula Funding in Context.* Boulder, Colo.: National Center for Higher Education Management Systems, forthcoming.
Leslie, L. L. "Higher Education Tax Allowances." *Journal of Higher Education,* 1976, *47,* 497-522.
Leslie, L. L. "Alternatives for Financing Higher Education Facilities." *Planning for Higher Education,* 1980, *8,* 15-22.
Leslie, L. L. "Selecting Responses to Fiscal Stress." Paper presented to the New Mexico State University Faculty Senate, Las Cruces, New Mexico, October 1983.
Miller, J. L., Jr. *State Budgeting for Higher Education: The Use of Formulas and Cost Analysis.* Michigan Governmental Studies, no. 45. Ann Arbor: University of Michigan Institute of Public Administration, 1964.
Wildavsky, A. *The Politics of the Budgetary Process.* (2nd ed.) Boston: Little, Brown, 1974.

Larry L. Leslie is professor of higher education and director of the Center for the Study of Higher Education at the University of Arizona.

Index

A

Alabama, cost calculations in, 33
Alabama Commission on Higher Education, 29, 42
Allen, R. H., 2, 3, 25, 26, 28, 32, 40, 42, 45-65, 91-93
Allocational budget formula, as incentive financing model, 48-50
Alternative costing procedures, and formula budgeting, 4
Althouse, P. R., 74, 76-77, 86
American Association of University Professors, 71
Andringa, R. C., 96
Anthony, R. N., 10, 18
Aquinas College, and reduction in size, 70
Arizona, University of, annual conference papers from, 96-98
Attrition: across-the-board, 73; selective, 75

B

Bacharach, S. B., 12, 18
Balderston, F. E., 72, 74-75, 84
Baldridge, J. V., 12, 18, 45, 64
Base amount, and cost calculations, 33
Baughman, G. W., 33, 41, 42-43, 97
Benefit-cost analysis, as allocation strategy, 7, 9, 10
Bennet, R. F., 96
Berdahl, R., 15, 18
Berg, D. J., 9, 14, 18
Board of Regents (Texas), 54, 64
Boggs, J. H., 76, 86
Bogue, E. G., 53, 64
Boutwell, W. K., 27, 43
Bowen, F. M., 71, 72, 73, 74, 84-85, 94
Bowen, H. R., 31, 43, 70, 86, 96
Boyer, E., 96
Braybrooke, D., 8, 18
Brinkman, P. T., 2, 3, 21-44, 61, 64, 89-91
Brown, B., 97
Budgeting: and conditions of decline, 67-86; formula, 21-44
Buffering, in formula budgeting, 30-31
Bundy Aid Program, 53

C

California: budgeting by formula in, 22, 29; buffering in, 30; control and incentives in, 16; cost calculations in, 32; flagship institution in, 34; responses to financial stress in, 73, 74, 94
California Postsecondary Education Commission, 98
Cameron, K., 9, 15, 18
Caruthers, J. K., 15, 18, 25, 27, 43
Central control, as incentive financing model, 47-48
Cohen, M. D., 8, 18, 55, 64
Colorado: incentive financing in, 2, 58-63, 64, 93; reallocation in, 69
Colorado at Boulder, University of, and incentive financing, 61, 93; and reallocation, 69
Colorado Commission on Higher Education, 58, 59, 61, 62, 65
Colorado State University, and incentive financing, 61
Conant, J. B., 13
Control: central, 47-48; and resource allocation, 16
Cost calculations, improved, in formula budgeting, 31-33, 91
Cost reimbursement, as allocation model, 7, 10-11
Curry, D. J., 47, 65, 97, 99
Curtis, D. V., 64
Cyert, R. M., 12, 18

D

Decision-support systems (DDS), in investment model, 10
Decoupling, and formula budgeting, 30

101

Decrements: across-the-board, 73-74; selective, 75-78
Dickmeyer, N., 73, 85
Dickson, W. J., 48, 65
Diesing, P., 12, 18
Domain defense, as allocation strategy, 7, 15
Dougherty, E. A., 72, 73, 83, 85

E

Ecker, G., 64
Enarson, H. L., 11, 18
Enrollment, trends in, 69
Every tub concept, as allocation strategy, 7, 13
Exxon Foundation, 2

F

Faculty, consultation with, in resource allocation, 83-84
Fayol, H., 48, 65
Fenker, R. M., 13, 18
Financing. *See* Incentive financing
Fischer, N. M., 65, 99
Fischer, W., 62, 65
Fixed costs, and cost calculations, 33
Florida: buffering in, 30; centers of excellence in, 34; cost calculations in, 33; cost reimbursement formula in, 11; quality improvement in, 35
Folger, J., 34-35, 43
Ford Foundation, 2
Formula budgeting: as allocation strategy, 7, 10-11; analysis of, 21-44; background on, 21-22; complexity in, 33-34; concept of, 21; criteria for evaluating, 24-25; data needs for, 40-41; defined, 23-24; evaluating effects of, 41-42; future of, 39-40; history of, 22-23; implications of, 40-42; new strategies for, 29-40; overall picture of, 39; and quality issue, 34-35; reasons for change in, 22; starting anew with, 35-39; strengths of, 25-26; synthesis of, 89-91; weaknesses of, 26-29
Fortunato, R. J., 71, 85
Freeman, T., 9, 18
Full-responsibility model, of incentive financing, 51-52, 58-63, 92. *See also* Responsibility-center budgeting
Furman, J., 72, 85

G

Gaither, G. H., 25, 26, 27, 44
Georgia: formula budgeting in, 29; quality improvements in, 35
Glenny, L. A., 71, 72, 73, 74, 84-85, 94
Goals, as allocation model, 7, 8-9
Good management practices, as incentive financing model, 51, 56-58, 92
Gray, J. A., 71, 85
Greene, C., 24, 43
Gross, F. M., 22, 24, 27, 32, 43

H

Hale, J. A., 25, 26, 27, 43
Halstead, D. K., 24, 25, 43, 53-54, 65
Hambrick, D. C., 48, 65
Hammond, M., 74, 85
Harcleroad, F. F., 96
Hartmark, L. S., 98
Harvard University, every tub model at, 13, 96
Health maintenance organizations (HMOs), and allocation strategy, 7, 13
Hewitt, C. N., 97
Heydinger, R. B., 78, 85, 99
Hoenack, S. A., 9, 14, 18
Hruby, N. J., 70, 85
Hyatt, J., 96
Hyde, W., 58, 60, 62, 63, 65, 98
Hyer, G., 97

I

Ihrig, W. E., 74, 85
Illinois, formula budgeting in, 29
Incentive financing: analysis of, 45-65; applications of, 52-63; background on, 45-46; conclusion on, 63-64; models for, 46-52; synthesis of, 91-93
Incentive planning, as allocation strategy, 7
Incentives, overall, 14
Incentives structuring, as allocation model, 7, 12-14, 16

Indiana: cost calculations in, 32; formula budgeting in, 22; marginal costing in, 11
Interest-group bargaining, as allocation model, 7, 12, 15, 16, 17
Investment, as allocation model, 7, 9–10

J

Jedamus, P., 69, 85
Johnson, M. D., 67, 85
Johnstone, W. A., 70, 85
Joint Budget Committee (Colorado), 58, 59, 61, 65
Jones, D. P., 23, 24, 25, 26, 43, 90, 98, 99
Jones, G., 97
Jones, L. R., 14, 18
Jons, T., 65, 99

K

Kaelke, M. E., 70, 86
Kansas, University of, across-the-board decrements at, 74
Karman, T. A., 76, 86
Keller, G., 9, 17, 18
Kentucky, formula budgeting in, 29, 35–38, 90, 91
Kentucky Council on Higher Education, 22, 35, 36, 37–38, 43
Kerr, C., 97
Key, V. O., Jr., 5, 18
Kotler, P., 8–9, 16, 18
Kreinin, M. E., 75, 85
Kruegar, D., 57, 58, 65

L

Lasher, W., 53, 54, 65
La Tourett, J. E., 77, 85
Lawler, E. J., 12, 18
Lee, J., 73, 85
Legislative Finance Committee (Montana), 29, 43
Leslie, L. L., 1–3, 22, 30, 43, 87–99
Lewin, K., 88
Lewis, V. B., 5, 19
Lilly Endowment, 2, 67, 98
Lindblom, C. E., 6, 8, 18, 19
Linear-behavior syndrome, and cost calculations, 32

Lott, G. B., 15, 18
Louisiana, cost calculations in, 33
Lozier, G. G., 74, 76–77, 86
Lusk, E. J., 10, 19

M

McClintock, D. L., 25, 43
McCoy, M., 53–54, 65, 97
McKeon, R. M., 48, 65
McKeown, M. P., 22, 24, 33, 34, 43
McKinney, D. L., 97
Madison, J., 11
Management by objectives (MBO), as allocation strategy, 7, 8
Management practices, good, as incentive financing model, 51, 56–58, 92
March, J. G., 6, 8, 12, 18, 19, 55, 64
Marginal costing: as allocation strategy, 7, 11; and cost calculations, 32–33
Marginal utility, as allocation model, 7, 9–10
Market interaction: as allocation assumption, 11–14; barriers to, 16; concept of, 6, 7; and rational calculation, 9; synthesis of, 88–89, 90, 91–92
Maryland: formula complexity in, 34; head counts of students in, 31
Mason, P. A., 48, 65
Meisinger, R. J., Jr., 11, 19, 23, 25–26, 29, 43
Melchiori, G. S., 71, 86
Michigan, University of, Priority Fund of, 76
Michigan State University: goal formulation bottom-up at, 9; selective attrition at, 75
Millard, R., 98
Miller, J. L., Jr., 23, 24, 25, 26, 27, 43, 90, 99
Millett, J. D., 25, 43–44
Millington, P., 75, 86, 97
Mingle, J. R., 37, 44, 71, 86
Minnesota: bulge funding in, 30; formula budgeting in, 29, 38–39, 90, 91; program review in, 78
Minnesota, University of, program review at, 78
Minter, J. W., 70, 86

Mintzberg, H., 48, 65
Mississippi, and centers of excellence, 34
Missouri: buffering in, 30–31; good-management-practices incentives in, 56
Missouri Department of Higher Education, 57
Montana State University, and reduction in size, 70
Morgan, A. W., 2, 3, 5–19, 87–89, 90, 91, 92, 94, 95
Mortimer, K. P., 2, 3, 67–86, 93–94, 98
Moss, C. E., 25, 26, 27, 44
Murphy, P. E., 8–9, 16, 18

N

National Institute of Education (NIE), 2
Nelson, R. R., 12, 19
New York: financial reversals in, 77; outcomes-oriented model in, 53
New York State Board of Regents, 78
Northeast Missouri State University (NMSU), good-management-practices incentives at, 56–58, 65
Northern Colorado, University of, and incentive financing, 63, 65

O

Oedel, L. P., 19
Office of Budgeting and Planning (Missouri), 57
Ohio: buffering in, 30; cost calculations in, 33; decrements in, 73–74; fixed- and variable-cost model in, 41
Ohio State University, across-the-board decrements at, 73–74
Oklahoma: formula budgeting in, 22; reallocation fund in, 76
Oklahoma State University, reallocation fund at, 76
Olsen, J. P., 8, 19
Oregon, formula complexity in, 34
Orwig, M., 25, 28, 43
Otto, H. L., 96
Otzenberger, S. J., 70, 86
Outcomes-oriented model, of incentive financing, 50–51, 53–56, 92

P

Pennsylvania: buffering in, 30; decentralization in, 13, 15, 96; decrements in, 74; target budgeting in, 76
Pennsylvania, University of, decentralized planning and budgeting at, 13, 15, 96
Pennsylvania State University: across-the-board decrements at, 74; variable budget targets at, 76
Performance budgeting, as allocation strategy, 7, 10
Perrin, J., 60, 65
Pfeffner, J., 12, 15, 16, 19
Pickens, W. H., 10, 19, 23, 27, 28, 31, 34, 44, 97, 98
Planning-Programming-Budgeting System (PPBS), as allocation strategy, 7, 8, 17, 18
Policy analysis movement, and resource allocation, 17
Porter, R., 19
Power relationships, in incentive financing, 46–47
Program reviews, for selective decrements, 77–78
Project on Reallocation, 79, 84

R

Rational calculation: as allocation assumption, 6–11; concept of, 6, 7; and market interaction, 14; prevalence of, 15–16; synthesis of, 88–89, 90, 91–92, 94
Rational-deductive idea, as allocation model, 7, 8–9
Rawson, T. M., 25, 26, 27, 43
Reallocation, institutional context of, 69–70
Reallocation funds, from selective decrements, 76–77
Reduction in size, institutional context of, 70
Resource allocation: additional sources on, 96–99; analysis of new strategies for, 5–19; assumptions at root of, 6–14; background on, 5–6; conclusions on, 17–18; and control, 16; discussion of, 14–16; and faculty consultation, 83–84; synthesis of, 87–89

Resource reduction and reallocation strategies: across-the-board, 72–74; analysis of, 67–86; attrition as, 73, 75; background on, 67–68; context and impact of, 79–80; decrements as, 73–74, 75–78; effectiveness of, 72–79; holistic view of, 84; institutional context of, 68–72; observations about, 79–84; program review for, 78–79; selective, 74–79; strengths and weaknesses of, 80–83; synthesis of, 93–94

Resources, reallocation of, 14–16

Responsibility-center budgeting, as allocation strategy, 7, 13, 95–96. *See also* Full-responsibility model

Retrenchment, institutional context of, 70–72

Riley, G. L., 64

Robl, R. K., 76, 86

Roethlisberger, F. J., 48, 65

Russell, J. D., 11

S

Salancik, G. R., 12, 15, 19

Schick, A., 11, 19

Schultze, R., 97

Scitz, C., 97

Shirley, R. C., 77, 86, 97

Simpson, W. A., 9, 18

Siren, R. L., 98

Smith, A., 11, 16

Spence, D. S., 30, 35, 38, 44

Stadtman, V. A., 69, 86

Standard budget targets, for selective decrements, 76

Stanford University, selective attrition at, 75

State Council of Higher Education (Virginia), 54, 65

State Education Department (New York), 53, 65

State University of New York (SUNY) at Albany, program review at, 77, 78–79

State University of New York (SUNY) at Binghamton, program review at, 77, 78–79

Strategic planning: as allocation strategy, 7, 8–9; and resource allocation, 17

Students, head counts of, in formula budgeting, 31

Study Committee on Public Higher Education Finance (Georgia), 29, 35, 44

Stumph, W. J., 25, 44

Summers, F. W., 25, 44

T

Task Force on the Future Funding of Post-Secondary Education (Minnesota), 29, 38, 44

Taylor, B. E., 2, 67–86, 93–94

Temple University, and reallocation, 69–70

Tennessee: buffering in, 30; formula complexity in, 34; performance budgeting in, 10, 35, 53

Texas: cost calculations in, 33; endowment program in, 53–56, 64, 93; flagship institution in, 34; formula budgeting in, 22, 29; outcomes orientation in, 53, 54, 56

Texas, University of, Regents' Endowed Teachers and Scholars Program of, 53–56, 64, 93

Texas A&M, and outcomes-oriented incentives, 53

Texas at Austin, University of, outcomes-oriented incentives at, 54, 56

Thompson, R. K., 77–78, 86, 97

Tierney, M., 2, 3, 67, 70, 76, 86, 98

Tompkins, L. D., 74, 85

Topping, J. R., 32, 40, 42

Truman, D. B., 12, 19

Twain, M., 45

U

United Kingdom, University Grants Committee (UGC) in, 15

Utah: revenues and enrollments in, 2; year-end balances in, 16

Utah, University of, 2

V

Vanderbilt University, responsibility-center budgeting at, 96

Virginia: funding floors in, 31, 33; funds for excellence in, 35; outcomes-oriented incentives in, 53, 54

W

Waddell, D. G., 71, 85
Washington, financial reversals in, 77–78, 84
Washington, University of: faculty consultation at, 84; program review at, 77–78
Weathersy, G. B., 30, 35, 38, 44
Weber, M., 47, 65
Whalen, E., 98
Wildavsky, A., 6, 12, 16, 17, 19, 90, 97, 99
Wilson, R. A., 96
Wisconsin, cost reimbursement formula in, 11
Wisconsin System, University of, 26, 44

Y

Young, M. E., 33, 41, 42–43

Z

Zemsky, R., 13, 14, 19
Zero-based budgeting (ZBB), as allocation strategy, 7, 10, 18